words about me*n* hits you in your heart, your gut, your soul. These pages invite you into exploring your deepest feelings and your most personal experiences—all reflected by the profoundly private and intimate stories of Lindy's own life.

At its core, *words about* me*n* is a book about one woman's most important, most intimate, most loving relationship: the one with her Self. And through her story home to that Self, she is inviting you and lovingly challenging you to deepen your own.

Lindy's poetic words bring you into a magical trance where you can't help but see and feel yourself reflected. You will need to pause to digest it all, and still feel hungry for more.

words about me*n* dares you into choosing the life that awaits you when you stop living for any other and, finally, choose to live the life that has called to your deepest, truest, freest Self since the very day you were born.

— Emma Heywood, Hypnotherapist to Wimbledon
and Australian Open Athletes

words about *me*n

words about *men*

lindy ehemann

intentional trips

ISBN-13: 979-8-9956753-0-3
library of congress control number: 2026909868

cover design by lindy ehemann

an intentional trips publication
intentionaltrips.com

it was never supposed to be about love.

if there was anything of which i was determined, it was that this life of mine would never be defined by the status of my relation to any other. that *love* was never the thing that would drive me. adventure, exploration, self-discovery, yes. but never love. love seemed a thing the world obsessed over and lost years of their lives to. lost their imaginations to. their drive, their spark, their raison d'etre. the people who chased love above all else seemed utterly wasted in their attempts to track down whatever fairytale image they'd imprinted in their minds only to be disappointed, time and time again, by reality. this notion of finding prince charming and living happily ever after had, my entire life, smelled entirely rancid.

no, i had bigger plans. loftier dreams. i was adamant about chasing all the highs life had to offer, of experiencing every single thing i could squeeze into however many years this life would grant me.

i came to this life to follow the oftentimes screeching call of my own soul and to know, from earliest breath, that i was here to save myself. to live an existence that cast out the bleak and summoned the holy. to bring myself back from the darkest depths i had entered, so early in life, that had led me to nearly escaping the mortal realm at the age of twelve.

the voice i had heard in my heart, even in that darkest night, that urged *stay alive. stay here. it will all be worth it. but you, angel, you must choose* to live.

from before memory even remembers remembering, a ferocity burned within me that rattled through my bones: *this life is my own.*

and this life demands to be fully experienced.

to share it with another—in the way that movies and society and so many of the girls i never fit in with seemed to lead me to believe i was meant to desire above all else—felt entirely a cage. a waste.

how wrong i was. how naive not to see that love is all it's ever been about. all that has ever mattered.

how right i was, knowing that love would never come in the packages that had been prescribed by the films and the laments of the girls whose dreams so differed from my own.

true human connection has always felt the most sacred of things to me—meeting people in the raw and the real. staring past the pleasantries and uncovering the marrow of our souls.

i have never known another way to befriend, to encounter.

and yet the understanding that every moment and friendship and person who crossed my hearts' path was all temporary and fleeting and part of the larger story of my life was something evident to me before i even had words to describe it. it was something that i felt in my cells, even when it pained me: *we are here for each other in a time and a place, and we can allow that to be beautiful.*

in a world that teaches you to cling onto people and places and moments and to size up and distill down every person who casts you a glance as a possible *husband*, there are few places for someone when they seek love without the need for it to fit into these prepackaged boxes.

this burning desire for depth and connection drove me and manifested itself in some of the most beautiful stories and friendships and lovers and moments a person could hope to know in this life.

and there were times when my inability to see clearly what it was that was even driving me—and how different that was from the rest of what everyone else seemed to want—landed me in worlds where i inflicted heartache on those undeserving and misery on myself for attaching to what was never mine to attach to.

the manner in which i love and have loved is the simplest truth of my being, and yet putting it to words has been the hardest part of this book to write—this thing within me that loves so deeply and feels so strongly and cares so much about each and every human who has ever come in contact with me and that has simultaneously never sought to keep them, except when the talons of my insecurity latched onto them in ways that left scars on us both.

i recognize now, that all i ever yearned for was unconditional love. love that is allowed to exist exactly as it is. no pretense, no outside pressure. no thoughts of what things *should* or *could* be.

just love.

friend, lover, partner, parent, self—it does not matter.

love is simply the act of allowing what is to be, and reveling in it with another. it is honesty and care, compassion and presence. it is unadulterated acceptance of all that is true.

and that is all i have ever sought from anyone who has crossed my path.

the journey to fully understanding that simplicity was a long one, that required both the acceptance of it in myself and the finding of others capable of holding it, too.

that journey is the one we are about to embark on together.

it is the story of me, told through the story of them.

i need you to know, dear stranger, that each of the men laid before you in this book have beauty and wonder all their own. yes, even the ones who will make you seethe.

i need you to know, dear stranger, that each of the humans you are set to encounter has their own story to tell, about both our time together and the greater tale of their lives, in which my existence was merely a moment.

i need you to know, dear stranger, that of every story you will read, to this day i believe only one of these men infiltrated me the way the deepest love ever truly can.

i need you to know, dear stranger, that he is the only one who i have ever considered myself to be *with* in any societal understanding of the term. that the rest of these men i existed alongside, untethered to, however deeply we may have been intertwined.

i need you to know, dear stranger, that while you will read of many people who have danced through my life, these words are about no one but me.

these words are about me.

these words are about men.

these words are about you.

these words are a mirror of every feeling, fleeting and festering.

these words have nothing to do with anyone but us.

these words have nothing to do with anything but the journey through.

these are not metaphors

these are the words

exactly as they happened.

the moments themselves

writing the poetry

without even trying.

no, it was never supposed to be about love.

but i need you to know, dear friend, that love is the only thing it was ever
going to be about.

for all of you.

yes, even you.

i still love you.

for years people would ask if i had a boyfriend and when i said no they would tell me there was still time and not to worry. as though i was the one of us who was worried. as though i was the one who had reduced our conversation to the level of assuming my worth was based on whether or not someone else was attached to me like a fifty-ton weight. they would say *but you're so great*, as though i was unaware. as though my *greatness* could only be validated by my relation to someone else. they would say they couldn't believe no one had snatched me up. as though i was some agentless, helpless flower waiting to be kidnapped and brought to life.

for years these interactions made my blood boil.

i did not come to this life to settle.
i did not pull myself back from the brink of blackest death and fight for the rights to my own happiness to turn around and attach it to someone who has not waged war for theirs.
i do not give a fuck about partnership for the sake of partnership.
if you have not fallen madly in love with your own existence in this life, there is not an atom of space for you in mine.

as a little girl i did not once dream of a white dress. i did not once dream of a white picket fence.

i dreamt of freedom. and of burning the world to the ground.

i did not come to this life to be your light.

i came here to be my own.

12

1

spring 2010

madison, wi

and, almost, your island

for #1, who taught me passion

spring 2010

madison, wi

17 july 2010

westchester, ny

the most erotic moment of my life to that point

was when we sat on your couch talking about life

　　and, staring at each other,

　　passed that lollipop back and forth between us.

i'd never known passion before

but you taught it to me in every late-night conversation

and every single text message

that slammed into my chest

　　like a battering ram.

i'm sorry i didn't come to see you on the island that summer.

and i'm sorry i lied to you about why.

to be honest

i don't remember what i told you.

but the truth was, i was so scared of how i'd felt for you.

and so scared of how intensely my mind

had blocked you out

　　as soon as you weren't in front of me.

and i was afraid of having sex with you

because i wanted to have sex with you

but i was scared i didn't know how.

i'm sorry for not telling you it was my first time.

but it was my first time.

and i'm sorry i didn't tell you that the day i was supposed to leave
new york and come to you
i was crying hysterically in the food court of a mall in white plains.
thinking, at nineteen, that if i was too afraid to get on that bus
it would mean i was too broken for love
for the rest of my life.

i want you to know that no one else has ever
looked in my eyes the way you did.
with a gaze that said it knew
every single thing
i needed someone to see.

and i want you to know that the way you called me *you* has stayed
with me all these years.

and i want you to know how afraid i was of how i felt for you.
and i'm sorry for being afraid of how i felt for you.

and i want you to know that i held out hope we'd find each other in europe for a long time. not in a way that hurt me. just in a way that, well, wouldn't that have been nice?

and i want you to know that it took everything in me not to touch you those times you came back.

and i want you to know i am so happy for you.
and i have such love for you.
and that you still come to visit me in dreams, from time to time.
with a gentleness that could only come from a soul
that my own had felt so truly loved
    and seen
    and held by.

spring 2010
madison, wi

there's a scar on the inside of my right wrist from the night we sat on your futon and tried to ignore the gravitational pull of our souls toward one another. from when i dug my nails into my own flesh so deeply i almost stopped myself from feeling the weight of all you said to me.

almost.

nineteen years old; terrified of how strongly every fiber of me wanted to be known by every fiber of you. only able to balance my desire for you with the self-inflicted pain that kept some part of me on this earth.

some part of me in my body.

nails dug so deep, locking me in me

rather than risk

    me

        being lost

  in you.

nails dug so deep there's a scar there fourteen years later.

do you have any idea how deep you have to dig, to leave a scar like that?

but that's how it always was with you.

or maybe that's how it's always been with me.

if i'm going to feel it, let me feel it all. even if it scars.

even if it never had to.

self-inflicted, all of it.

commemorating each moment that plucked the chords of my heart like a guitar and reverberated through me.

i cannot let this feeling pass me by. cannot let this moment go.

riddle me with lines and bumps and bruises; cover me in a map of how i got here.

let this life exist as homage to the moments that made me.

raptured; deep; nails-dug-in the whole way.

13 june 2012

prague

we rarely spoke, after i didn't come to see you on the island that summer. and i know that was entirely on me. i had held you at a distance from the moment you had gotten closer to me than any human ever before. i gave you almost nothing because i was terrified that giving you anything at all would mean giving you every single thing i had, and those were stakes i could not risk gambling with.

two years after the spring we'd spent in secret, i was living out the european summer we had dreamed of together in endless conversations of the lives we may someday live. after a semester in paris that had stripped me down and sown me back together and galvanized me in ways i never could have fathomed, you messaged me to ask how i was faring. to see what wonders my heart had found.

your questions were deep and my replies were short, because we still were who we'd always been.

but then we began, once more, to muse on the future. on the endless possibilities, and the paths less traveled. i mentioned my graduation, only a year away now. no idea what life would hold for me on the other side. and you, understanding in a way no one else could, said *that's the best feeling though. knowing that you can't predict what your life will be, what you will do.*

life should never be a straight line.

you had always feared a life lived in a straight line.

and i had always revered that commitment to waywardness about you.

and—twenty-one years old, prophetic as ever—i replied,

i've always kind of known i'll never do anything conventional.

and paris just reaffirmed that. i'd rather be the person with no solid career path at 30 because i've traveled the world and had a dozen unique odd jobs, than be the one who never left the mediocre corporate america job they got right after graduation.

and you, speaking truth to the pieces of me you had loved since we met, said *that's part of what has always made you one of my favorite people.*

and your words sent starbursts through my entire body and made my heart catch her breath, the very same way they had all those moons before.

and then i changed the subject. the very same way i would, all those moons before.

because, even two years later, i still could not handle

being seen

    and recognized

    and reflected

so sincerely

by someone who i loved

    so deeply,

it all but

    paralyzed me

    with fear.

25 october 2014

suburbs, chicago

the night our mutual friends got married we stayed up later than everyone else, just like we always had. drunk but not wasted, just like we always were. kneeling at the edge of a hotel bed. off it, not in it. just like we'd always done.

well, almost always.

just talking. like we always did.

it had been over four years since the spring you had changed me and here you were, looking in my eyes again the way you always had. the way no other man has ever truly looked at me. the way you knew i was the only one who could see.

you told me you still wondered. still thought about it. still imagined what might have been, if i'd come to the island that summer.

like i was supposed to.

like we had planned.

1 september 2018
lincoln park, chicago

i have a panic attack hours before the wedding, but it doesn't even occur to me that maybe i shouldn't go. i'd made a special request for a vegan option by writing *vegan, if possible* under the word *vegetarian* on the rsvp, and the second i'd dropped it into the postbox my stomach had fallen out of my body at my own *audacity* to make such requests at a wedding of someone who i had hardly spoken to in eight years. at the *guilt guilt guilt* i felt over the fact that you'd had to message me to ask if i was coming, because i had taken so long to send in that tiny little rsvp.

the truth was, whether or not i was coming had never been in question.

and the truth was, the fact that you'd invited me after all that time had meant more to me than i could ever possibly begin to tell you.

but the truth was, the man i was with at the time *just didn't understand why* i would want to go to *your* wedding.

what a gift, to still be loved so wholly by you that you want me there, i had thought.

traitor traitor traitor was all he could see.

i knew he was wrong and i knew it was special and i knew i wanted to be there for you and with you on that day, but every hour that it grew closer he grew wearier and my heart could not hold his shame and his jealousy and his disdain although i did not have those words for it at the time.

on the way to your ceremony i found myself drinking an old fashioned at the chicago diner with the same friend who had sat with me in that food court in white plains eight years before, as i had sobbed and confessed i was too paralyzed by fear to go to the island to see you. and here i was, twenty-seven now, hyperventilating again as, once more, she held me and told me *you do not have to go you do not have to go you do not have to go.*

but i knew, this time, i had to go.

she came downtown with me and sat at a restaurant across the street for hours in case i could not breathe. *you can leave you can leave you can leave* she had told me and i knew i could and i knew i wanted to do everything in my power to be there with you on that day.

i wondered all night how well i concealed it, and the truth is i have no clue and the truth is you had much more important things to be tuned into that night than whether or not i seemed *off*.

but it's worth confessing, here and now, that i did breathe all through that night. that i calmed enough in your joy and your wife's warmest welcome and the love that permeated it all to find my feet below me and dance until the very last song.

when dinner ended, you told me to tell my friend to come and join us. she left the restaurant she'd been sitting guard at for hours and showed up in the pure white sundress i'd lent her that morning without ever considering she would be wearing it as she crashed your wedding. she stole the suit jacket of the only other man we knew there and we all danced like wildlings together and my heart soared with peace.

it's prophetic, looking back, the tonic that your warmth and her support and the stamping of legs into dancefloor for hours on end provided.

the antidote to the projected shame i was allowing myself to carry.

the recipe for my eventual release.

23 february 2022
puerto viejo, costa rica

you've been on my mind lately and i don't know why because we haven't really spoken in over a decade but i can't stop thinking about what we shared and i write a poem about it and three days later you message me for the first time in forever telling me your mom lives in the same tiny town as me in a country four thousand miles away from where you're from and suddenly the fact that your energy has been everywhere makes sense and suddenly the fact that your energy has been everywhere is crazy.

there's a scorpion in my kitchen sink and i don't know how to relay to you over the expanse of time and space and your wife and baby and life that seems so beautiful and so normal that i'm having conversations with our ghosts in a hut in the jungle in the town your mom lives in in a country four thousand miles away. don't know how to convey to you that it means nothing but it means everything and you are still with me but not like that just that you're here and hi and did you feel it too?

that somehow, across everything, you are still here.
and hi.
and i'm glad you feel it, too.

2010

2011

2

july 2011

michigan

for #2, who taught me we can't always see

july 2011
lawton, michigan

it was more than a trillion lifetimes ago now, but at the end of that summer, our friend and her friend came to visit me in madison and as the beers flowed it came out that the friend of our friend and i had both spent nights with you that year. one of us said *i think he stole my underwear* and the other said *holy shit, me too* and we laughed harder than i had laughed in ages and i've always wondered if it was insane coincidence or if you really did have a thing for it.

she lives in peru, now. she works with sacred medicine and holds ceremony for westerners to come and meet the spirits of the forest and heal their hearts. it's funny, how she and i kind of ended up living these parallel lives that really have nothing to do with each other except that i have spoken to the forests and the plants and the spirits, too. and that we both lived in costa rica for a while and bathed in the same wild pools. and that we both have these lines that trace back to you and your possibly-underwear-stealing ways and that tiny lake in southwestern michigan. that summer when we were both sorority girls who were never supposed to be sorority girls, with our hearts that yearned for something greater than summers on manmade lakes and drunken revelations.

it's funny how, in thinking of you, i inevitably think of her. how much we had in common and how much i always held her on this pedestal where i never believed i belonged. how we both orbited the same worlds and overlapped in so many ways and yet i just couldn't see it.

i wonder, now, if you ever think about us, if you even know where we are.

the two jungle girls whose underwear you may have stolen in the summer of twenty eleven. the wild ones whose hearts ran free.

those two kids, who traded in the manmade lakes and the lakemade boys and the drunken summers of the midwest for the waterfalls and the shamans and the becoming of who they knew they could be; the discovering of terrain yet untamed.

2010

2011

2012

3

july 2011 – winter 2012

wisconsin

los angeles

for #3, who tried to teach me

that i

am not

special

7 may 2011

madison, wi

his nickname was voldemort and that really should have been more of a red flag. he got under my skin through my open wounds and he pried them apart while telling me on repeat to stop doing this to myself. i'd never known sadism in someone that way, so i really did believe somehow i was the one insane. *madness madness madness* being given a mile and having it claimed as an inch. *insanity insanity insanity* being given an inch and having it claimed for a mile. he loved torture in a way they make documentaries about and the fact that he was *your* best friend should have been more of a red flag too.

that you would treat me, in the end, as lifelessly as he had.

but before you convinced me to give you my body, you were my friend. and before you made me crazier than he ever had, you understood.

his treatment of me had put a rift between the two of you and it had been eighteen months of his torment and while it had lightened that year he still loved to play with his food. and i was ripe for the feast.

there was a month left in classes and you asked me to formal and it was supposed to be the most fun we'd ever have and two of my best friends made the trip up for it and i was so excited to show them my life.

and i guess, in the end, i did show them my life.

if i'm honest i don't even remember what he said but he was prying me apart in only the way he could, in that sadistic way where anyone who didn't know wouldn't be able to see. sitting there at dinner, surrounded by friends. acid in wound after wound and i was shrinking ever smaller while trying not to break. everyone oblivious to the slaughter except for him and me and you.

the part of you that loved me more than him, the part of you that knew good even if you claimed you could never see it, the part of you that had been pulled apart your whole life, too—that part of you snapped. right there in your suit and tie at the table with all our friends, you slammed your knife straight through your porcelain plate and screamed at him. and a room full of drunk frat boys had never gone quiet so fast. every eye on us and you fighting my battles that no one even knew i was waging.

i don't remember if i cried in that instant or if i lasted long enough to make it to the bathroom but i do know the breaking of that plate broke something in me.

i was livid with you for defending me and livid with you for making a scene and livid with myself for needing to be saved at all.

it took me years to come to terms with the fact that you went from my savior from him to treating me worse than him in the span of two months. how you spent years being my friend and weeks burning it all to the ground. how the worst of it was that you did just what he did, in the end:

poured gasoline all over something real and told me the inferno was not only my own doing,

      but that the fire only existed

         in my mind.

july 2011
madison, wi

i ask you not to touch my left shoulder and you get mad at me for all the *rules* i have. how i don't like kissing you and i've never once come for you and how i try to hide my body from you even when you are inside of it. i tried to show you my scars and all you did was tell me how inconvenient it was that they still ruled me. you told me to stop hurting myself but not in the way that comes from love, just in the way that says *grow the fuck up*.

after two years of friendship you knew where every single weakness in me lay because i had trusted you to see it all and the darkest irony is that trusting you to see it all allowed me to trust you to see even more but the moment you were granted access to my bed you flipped those wounds on their heads and made me feel like a fool for believing you would still hold them once you'd finally gotten ahold of the body

in which

they dwelled.

three

summer 2011 – winter 2012

everywhere

i told you you could fuck whoever you wanted, as long as it wasn't her. said i couldn't explain why, but she made my skin crawl and out of respect for me just please don't go there. out of respect for our friendship, just don't put your fucking dick inside the one person who put me on edge in a way i could not yet explain.

and those were the rules.

use a fucking condom while you're out pulling strangers.

and don't. fuck. her.

truth be told if you broke the latter within weeks i'm sure you broke the former even sooner.

the two of you started spending more time together. baking cupcakes and having movie nights and suddenly after two years of never speaking you'd become best friends.

i told you it made me uneasy and you called me *crazy*.

not an insinuation.
not a fill in the blank.
you used the word.

crazy.

again and again.

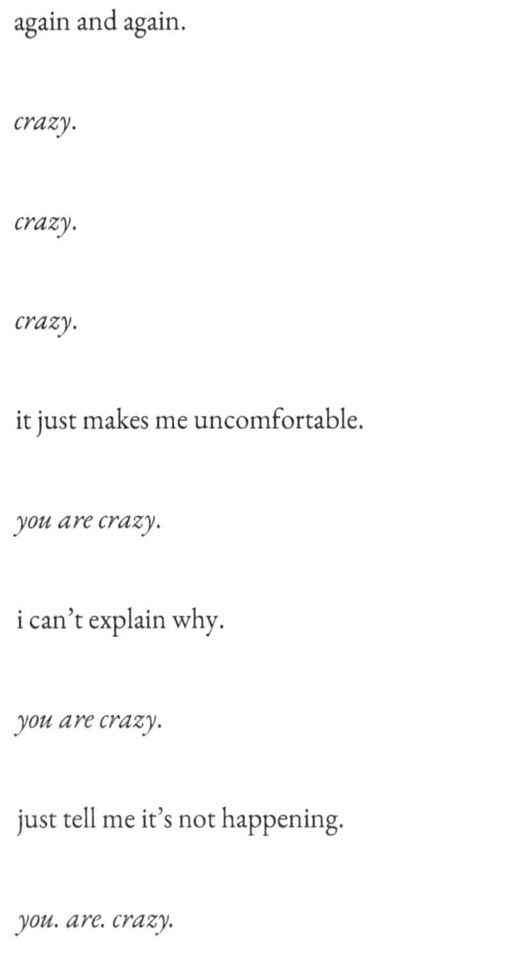

crazy.

crazy.

crazy.

it just makes me uncomfortable.

you are crazy.

i can't explain why.

you are crazy.

just tell me it's not happening.

you. are. crazy.

and so crazy i went as i betrayed my sanity, convincing my gut she was wrong and my heart she was blind. all the while giving you access to my body in a way i had never given anyone and all the while telling myself *maybe this is what it's supposed to feel like.*

there was a day i'd gone so *crazy,* i even asked her. the knowing in me driving so strongly that even my terror of confrontation couldn't stand in my way. i said to her, point blank, *is there anything going on with you two?*

and she looked at me, point blank, and oathed the words *i would* never. *do that. to you.*

so *crazy*, i continued to believe, i must have been.

but mid-august came and a friend brought it up. he'd thought that i'd known, but the second he saw my face change when he casually mentioned the two of you, he realized. do you have any idea what kind of look that must have been? to, in one instant, feel destroyed and betrayed and vindicated and *crazy* and sane and stabbed and pathetic and a fool and somehow relieved all at once.

to know i was right.

and to know what that being right then meant.

the fallout was brutal and everyone knew and of all the things i felt, forever unwantable is the one that wrapped her talons most deeply in my soul. never enough, never worthy of care.

the putrid thing is, i kept fucking you for months. drove out to that stupid house in sun prairie you'd rented a room in after graduating. let you teach me how to drive stick after we broke into your office at midnight and had sex in the board room. flew to la once you'd moved there and we went to fucking disneyland and my mind can't even comprehend it now, how much i hated myself. how i could see it was rancid clearly enough to not tell a soul what i was doing, for fear of how they'd react to the idea of me still even speaking to you, let alone sharing your bed.

yet i clung to the rot in the hopes it would save me.

maybe it's pathetic and maybe it's sad or maybe it's just textbook stockholm syndrome, somehow feeling like the bottomless cavern you'd created in me could only be sown shut by the reaper himself.

i failed a class that semester. had a gpa of 1.75. a lifetime on the honor roll and there i was, staying up until 6am not writing midterm papers and spiraling in anxiety to the point that i just never went to that class again. couldn't even face the professor let alone utter the word *help*. my grades were so bad the university almost didn't let me study abroad the next semester.

and i never told anyone that. could never bring myself to admit how deep that shame had taken me. how much your callousness had destroyed me. how the despair i felt in the wake of that summer almost lost me a dream i had held since i was eleven years old.

instead i just kept showing up, day after day. counting the seconds until i would leave the country and be lightyears away from this. smile in place, beer pong ball in hand. secretly texting you from the frat house basement.

mistaking the blackness of your attention
    for the warm embrace
    of love.

three

he tells me i can't spend my whole life running and that i'll need to grow up someday and then he treats my body like it is a punching bag that exists only for his pleasure. he tells me how the other women he's fucking come for him at the slightest touch. he tells me i'm not special and for almost a year i allow myself to believe him. he tells me he is incapable of love and for some reason i want to prove him wrong but all that happens is that he proves himself right again and again and again. he tells me throwing up won't make me skinny and an hour later i am on my knees gagging on his body, praying someday i will be good enough for someone.

the day the spell breaks i am staring at his face on the screen of my laptop, spending a parisian spring evening inside, listening to his specious rants. he tells me the color green reminds him of me because of my eyes, and suddenly the pure comedy of all of it slaps me across the face harder than he ever did and i slam my laptop shut on the other side of the world and go outside to walk freely along the seine and i never respond to a text from him again.

two and a half years later i see him at the bar we'd spent years in together and he wants to go outside and *talk* and i laugh in his face, my best friend standing behind me, fists clenched ready to claw his eyes out. he tells me he needs resolution and i say that's great for you but i am done living for what you need. and all i feel inside is vindication.

and all i feel inside is strength.

and all i feel inside is terror.

and all i feel inside is done.

he has children now. a wife. a home.

he almost never crosses my mind. but when he does i wonder if he ever looks at his daughter.

and thinks of me.

and thinks of all of the women

he could not love.

three

a decade later and i realize
i've been clearing different men out
in every place
i return to.
and i realize
the next place
i have to go
is southern california
and suddenly my tongue
feels too big
for my mouth.

three

somehow the smell of lavender can still remind me of you. unexpected out of nowhere on nights like these when i'm spinning so hard that i drive to the fucking dollar store to buy discount candles so i can try to force relaxation in a strangers bathtub and label it self care and all i want is to turn my brain off so i tell myself *buy lavender buy lavender buy lavender* in the hopes that the chemical compounds will regulate my nervous system and pour this madness out of my head and down the drain and instead what happens is i light the first candle and the smell envelops me the way your body used to and of all the things i was expecting from this night, you were not it. distant, stirring blackness in the back of my mind. the memory attached to scent so faintly after all these years i can hardly even place it. all those months you told me i was nothing and i kept coming back to you because at least being your nothing felt like being something. more than a third of my life has passed since i've let you touch me and somehow here you are, enveloping me in this bathtub.

telling me

once more

that i

am not

special.

three

2011 – 2023
earth

you built cages
    out of words
and i let myself stay trapped
    behind verbal barbed wire
        for years

you've been watching my story lately. always one of the firsts. sitting there, on your phone in your house in rural wisconsin. wife and kids in the other room.

i wonder if you're happy for me.

i wonder if you see my dreams come true and laugh at me in callous vitriol.

you used to tell me i couldn't be peter pan and even then, even in the hellscape of shame you'd thrust me into, i knew you were full of mediocre, life-numbing, soul-draining shit. knew even then that a peter pan life had nothing to do with immaturity and everything to do with seizing every single moment to play and feel and live and see color even when the world and men like you tried to force it all to grey. knew even then that you were destined for a life of culver's drive-thrus and plastic wrapped monotony and reliving the glory days and making fun of the magic i made with the same boys you've called friends since before any of you were old enough to order a beer in those townie bars without your dad saying it was okay.

and maybe i'm wrong. maybe it is the former. that somehow you've grown enough to realize how fucking wrong you were. and how fucking wrong it was, what you did to me that summer. that maybe, somewhere inside you, you can somehow hope for my happiness while once having had veins that flowed with nothing but ice-nine.

and lord i pray no one ever treats your daughter

the way you treated me

    or her

        or her.

2010

2011

2012

4

june 2012

madison, wi

for #4, who taught me there are some friends
you're just not supposed to sleep with

june 2012

august 2013

madison, wi

it was The Weirdest Thing That Ever Happened and we didn't speak of it for over a year, except for sideways glances during games of Never Have I Ever with our friends. and for it being The Weirdest Thing That Ever Happened, i was so grateful you never actually made it weird. that life just kept going on for us, exactly as it had.

a month after The Weirdest Thing That Ever Happened, one of my best friends came to visit and the two of you had a Fling So Fun we all giggled about it for ages.

the summer after the Fling So Fun, i graduated and you took me out to dinner on the square a week before i left town and we shared a bottle of Good Wine and you asked me about my dreams and my plans and the world i was taking on. the world your engineering degree was keeping you one more year away from. you had picked a nice restaurant by adult standards and a *really nice* restaurant by college standards and you paid for everything because you said we were celebrating me and not a single one of my other friends had made an effort to celebrate me and that has always stuck with me. and sure we were all young and broke but it really had nothing to do with the niceness of the restaurant and everything to do with the fact that you really set an intention that night to make me feel special.

a glass of red wine in, you said something i don't quite remember but, cheekily, i replied *...like that time we had sex?*

and you set down your wine glass and kept your eyes on the table for an eternal second and then you smiled that mischievous smile you wore so well and tilted your blue eyes up at mine without lifting your head and said *you realize we have* never *once spoken about that, right?* and i said *yeah, because it was The Weirdest Thing That Ever Happened* and you raised your voice in excited agreement and said *it was The* Weirdest *Thing That* **Ever** *Happened.*

we both laughed for minutes straight about The Weirdness and about those fleeting moments in the last year on the Troll Hole porch where those games of Never Have I Ever were the closest we had ever come to acknowledging it and the time my mom had come to visit and made a comment about how cute you were and we both blushed more than we should have and about how you and my best friend and i had all giggled and giggled and giggled together about your Fling So Fun.

as the night moved on and the wine flowed, we found our way from the really nice restaurant by college standards to the oldest dive bar in the city and after lord knows how many drinks you told me you were in love with my best friend, and not the one you had had the Fling So Fun with. and you were so mad at her for how in love you were that you didn't know what to do.

there were so many ways i knew you so well, but that confession came out of complete left field. all the things we'd left unspoken had always been play, and here you were speaking truth to something that was rotting you from within.

how you'd loved her for years and how you were certain she knew and how you wanted to know my thoughts on it all and how i told you in truest sincerity that this moment was the first i'd ever heard of any of this.

when i told her the next day i watched her heart shatter as the reality of the friendship she thought she had with you dissolved in an instant. she'd never known how you felt and you could not believe that and all of it was just so complicated for something that never really existed.

the fallout from that conversation left none of us better—just a troupe of twenty-two-year-olds who could not handle unrequited love, no matter whose heart was involved. after fourteen months of our friendship surviving The Weirdest Thing That Ever Happened, a rift was sown in that friend group that would never be righted.

maybe it all would have dwindled with graduation, regardless. the paths diverging, the storylines changing. but it's always been interesting to me, how sometimes it's the things that didn't happen that end up destroying a friendship much more than the things that did.

2010

2011

2012

5

summer 2012

    and before, between, and since

wisconsin

        for #5, who taught me there are some friends
            you're just supposed to sleep with

        and in doing so, has taught me what it means
          to truly be loved as an equal

you had blacklisted every woman you'd ever walked away from

and the thought of a world without you was so terrifying

it almost stopped me from touching you.

    almost.

so i kept you at a distance

while keeping you in my bed

and allowed the doorways to a future

in which it was ever anything other than exactly what it was

      to remain closed.

and the thing is, that is exactly how it was ever supposed to be.

and i think you knew that long before i did.

or at least you embraced it

      more readily.

our endless dreams of lives of adventure and love and magic and play

and futures in which we were together but never *together.*

it all became an understanding

      that never even needed to be said aloud.

an understanding of understanding.

that sometimes something really is

      everything

      and nothing

      all at once.

2010

2011

2012

6

july 2012

michigan

> *for #6, who taught me the meaning of the lyrics*
> *"i've still got the rugburns on both my knees"*

two weeks later i still had the rugburns and we all went to a fundraiser and i was with him and you were with the woman my cousin set you up on a blind date with and one of my favorite pictures of myself is one where both you and him are with me and i'm wearing a fancy dress and holding a beer making a face that says *they don't know what i know.*

you ended up marrying that blind date and now you live in my hometown and have a summer house on the lake we first met at and it's just so funny, how it all ends up going.

our summers intersected so briefly and in the wake of all those wakes, your life became the one i was leaving behind.

you, with the spouse and the kids and the money and the houses in the places that raised me.

me, with myself and with him and not with him and with the shoestring budgets and the new homes in the infinite places that would raze me.

2010

2011

2012

5

summer 2012

and before, between, and since

wisconsin

chicago

*for #5, who taught me there are some friends
you're just supposed to sleep with*

*and in doing so, has taught me what it means
to truly be loved as an equal*

summer 2012
madison, wi
chicago

you let it be fun and i think that was the most cathartic thing about it all.

that, and the fact that, after the first night, you didn't start treating me like you had never once cared about me before the first night. that your love for me and demeanor toward me did not flinch simply because we had snuck out of the frat house at three am to go drunk naked swimming off the sorority house dock and had sex in the lake—just us and mucky toes and unaccounted for buoyancy and laughs that came from somewhere real. that you could go to fancy fundraisers out of town with me and lovingly make fun of me for taking us on the wrong train and still make me feel seen and heard and cared for. that you listened to the enormity of my dreams and believed in them and mirrored them with the immensity of your own.

that you taught me, just by your very being, what it felt like to be loved.

2010

2011

2012

2013

7

spring 2013

madison, wi

for #7, who taught me you can never undo a moment
where you failed to show love

spring 2013
madison, wi

i am so sorry
for how i handled

    everything.

you deserved so much better.

2010

2011

2012

2013

5

summer 2012

7 july 2013

and before, between, and since

wisconsin

chicago

wisconsin

for #5, who taught me there are some friends
you're just supposed to sleep with

and in doing so, has taught me what it means
to truly be loved as an equal

we probably should have set an alarm and we probably should have been more discrete and our friends probably should have given us more grief about it, if we're being honest.

but we didn't and we weren't and they held their tongues which is kind of shocking for them and in the end everyone got where they needed to be on time and in the end it really was worth it, don't you think?

2010

2011

2012

2013

2014

8

31 december 2013 – 27 june 2014

london

for #8, who taught me how to come.

and who also

taught me

how to go.

31 december 2013

london

an hour after the clock struck twelve, i find you in a sea of smoke and strangers on the frigid balcony of a random north london flat and say *do you want to go home and fuck and then pretend it never happened* and you grab my hand and we go home and get the first part right.

half a year spent holding you at a distance while i held you in my arms and somehow it was all so obvious to me until it wasn't. how much we both cared and how much we both carried and how much neither of us dared look at any of it.

i know i wasn't good to you and i know you weren't good to me either, except for the fact that we were both better to each other than anyone had ever been before. and it really was love, in the ways we were capable of letting it be at the time. in the ways that said it could only ever be disavowed and unacknowledged.

in the ways that said deny something real in defense of things more delicate.

it still does my head in, how we could be so honest with each other while never speaking a word that felt true. how you could let me in so closely and still shut out every single bit of sincerity. how i really did try, in the end, to set it all straight. but you wouldn't even acknowledge the things we carried existed, let alone their need to be set and straightened.

how we let the ocean of the unspoken brew a tempest so insidious,

neither of us could weather the unseen storm.

eight

winter 2014
shoreditch, london

we shared a darkness and it brought us together. a darkness i had spent
my entire life trying to escape. a darkness you had spent your entire life
denying
existed.

mildewy clothing will always be you. how your primark sweaters never fully dried on those council housing heaters. how the fire hazard of synthetic fabric on decades old radiators never even occurred to us. too drunk on everything we touched to even consider the possibility of it all going up in smoke.

but it was always destined to go up in smoke.

the cloud you'd surrounded yourself in, the first sign.

the cloud i'd enveloped you in, the second.

eight

2014

earth

for a year after you the smell of rollies turns me on and it feels like some kind of ironic cosmic torture. sweet, sticky tobacco hitting my nostrils on the street and suddenly some pavlovian reflex has me drifting to you. half a year spent watching you slowly kill yourself, conditioning my body to go down with you. never allowing myself to plummet to the depths of your darkness, but dancing close enough to the edge to see the sunlight fade.

how can something repel and attract in such equal measure?

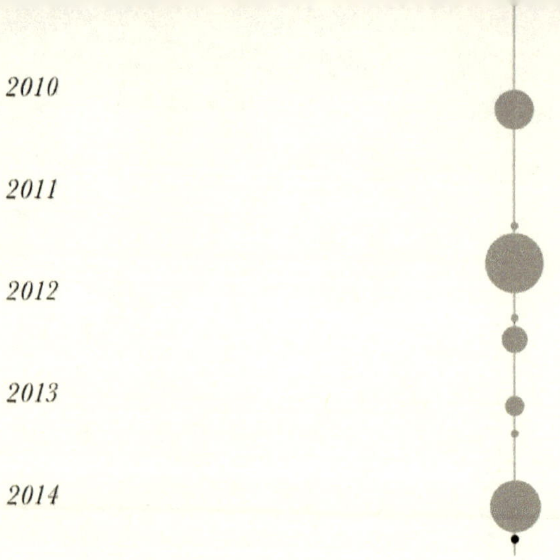

2010

2011

2012

2013

2014

9

august 2014

chicago

for #9, who taught me there is such a thing as bad sex

but really dude.

was it
your first time?

2010

2011

2012

2013

2014

2015

10

13 january – 9 march 2015

melbourne

> *for #10, who, through your deplorability,*
> *taught me self-respect*

ten

13 january – 9 march 2015

melbourne

her name was hannah and her boyfriend was a piece of shit and i slept with him. he said they weren't together at the time and he said she knew what was going on but the truth is i don't believe it now and the truth is i hardly believed it then. i had known them both in london and for knowing them both in london, i knew he was awful and i knew he was cruel. and for some reason i thought knowing these things about him would save me from them. for some reason i thought playing like i was in the boys' club would save me from the way i knew he treated girls. crude jokes and being *chill* and watching the footy and listening to *drake's* new album even though i didn't really get the hype.

but the truth is it actually was fun, until it wasn't.

and the truth is i did come away with some good stories.

and the truth is i really hope they weren't together that summer,

like he said

they kind of weren't.

and the truth is i pray she never took him back.

and the truth is i was twenty-three and hated myself.

and the truth is he was actually so abominable it forced me

into self-respect.

and the truth is, for that i am grateful.

because the truth is i have never allowed anyone

to treat me

the way he did

ever

again.

2010

2011

2012

2013

2014

2015

11

13 may 2015

melbourne

for #11, who taught me i'm not cut out

for one-night stands

13 may 2015

richmond, melbourne

i really wanted to never see you again because i had never done that before and it felt like a rite of passage and yet somehow you just lingered in my bed for hours the next morning until the point i had to leave and when i told you i was going you just kind of sat there silently for so long i invited you with me and my friends and then you just kind of added yourself to my life like it had never occurred to you that my whole intention was to forget your name.

but instead of forgetting your name we both just kind of forgot how we'd met and a few months later you were working at the bar with me and the centers of our venn diagrams were such that the tendrils weave, ever so lightly, to this day.

and it's funny, how things go.

you set out one night at twenty-four, intent on finding someone to never remember. and you wake up with a broken bedframe and a storyline you'll never forget.

2010

2011

2012

2013

2014

2015

5

summer 2012

7 july 2013

18 – 31 may 2015

   and before, between, and since

wisconsin

chicago

wisconsin

europe

     for #5, who taught me there are some friends
       you're just supposed to sleep with

     and in doing so, has taught me what it means
       to truly be loved as an equal

i always find myself in piazza navona at the turn of an irreversible tide.

at sixteen, at the start of a six-week journey through italy that would affirm a dream and a path in me that would never again be put to rest.

at twenty-one, reclaiming my sovereignty for the first of infinite times.

at thirty-one, finally accepting that the only way to step into my eternal future was to face the darkest demons of my past.

at thirty-three, where my feet carried me immediately after vanquishing the last shadow i'd hid from on earth. where i transitioned from *then* to *now*.

and, in the middle of it all, at twenty-four. with you.

half a year after i'd moved to australia the first time. back in the eternal city as i was realizing, once again, how much the reality i'd found myself in needed to change. back in our eternal existence together, realizing, once again, how much you had always been this barometer for how i was living life. seeing in me the potential i knew was there, the potential i simultaneously rose to and cowered in fear from. mirroring to me the things we both knew to be possible. each of us, unknowingly providing living proof that all we dreamed did, in fact, exist.

i can't stand in that piazza without feeling you, now. without plunging back into that night we snuck out of the airbnb we shared with my family at two am and danced with a troupe of gypsies on ponte sisto and eventually found our way to the piazza and fontana dei quattro fiumi.

it still blows my mind that no one else was around.

just us, and the piazza, and the fountain, and the decades of my ghosts who have been resurrected on that spot before and since.

7 july 2020

logan square, chicago

he calls me. one am his time. in the middle of one of those pandemic months where my reality was completely locked down but his, on an island on the other side of the world, was wide open. he's drunk and perusing the aisles of a 7-eleven and he calls me to ask what i'm *doing*.

he says it like an accusation.

because it is.

i tell him i'm figuring some things out and he pushes back. but what are you *doing*. he says my soul is meant to travel and make art and follow my dreams and i've been locked away in a tower for six months and what am i *doing*? to any other ears the conversation would sound ludicrous because where, oh where, would you have me go right now?

but i know he's right.

because i don't *know* what the fuck i'm *doing*.

all i know is nothing feels right.

that i've been throwing myself into anything and nothing but none of it worthwhile.

and all i've wanted for years is for someone to call and shake me and say *what the fuck are you doing?*

and here he is.

once again

prodding the potential in me

i was too terrified

    to explore

    myself.

piano man still reminds me of you. pants around our ankles, arms around your friends. swaying in time and belting the words together and living in moments the rest of the world simply observed. the utter joy and the promise to escape the fate of the characters of whose lives we sang.

all those times you let me into your other life. how you had another life. how we both always knew we needed other lives. how so often it felt like we were the only two who realized other lives were even possible.

you went on into yours and i went on into mine but the threads and the love and lines never severed. for a long time i did wonder if the paths would ever re-intertwine. all those meet ups and adventures and the trust that we would see each other again. someday.

and we have always seen each other again someday.

the trust that you living your other life and i living mine was the only way for it to ever be. how you were my first lesson in letting go in order to receive. how keeping you as it has all changed and shifted and moved has been one of the greatest blessings of my life. how you showed me what it meant to be truly accepted and loved and allowed to be free. and i still do not know if you could even conceive of another way to be.

you were the first one to set a bar, and even if i wavered in my own love for myself, the height you'd shown me ultimately remained.

how you, ultimately, remained.

even as everything and everyone else faded away.

and to this day—through continents and heartbreak and dreams come true and other lives lived—you love me in a way i could never express my truest gratitude for, you mirror me in a way that helps me see my own beauty, you trust me in a way that leaves no room for fear.

2010

2011

2012

2013

2014

2015

8

31 december 2013 – 27 june 2014

6 june 2015

london

for #8, who taught me how to come.

and who also

taught me

how to go.

i don't really remember much from that day with you, the time i came back. just that you showed up as the version of you i had glimpsed barely enough times to know existed. the one i'd spent half a year holding out hope would turn up again, even when i'd seen no sign of him for months.

and that was a relief. because i really had started to wonder if it had ever been real at all, the light that moved through your shadows. but there, on that sunny london morning—a year after the night i cried on the kitchen floor while you fucked a woman whose scars matched my own in your tiny bedroom down the hall—you turned up on regents canal and you were the you i had always known could exist. the you i so desperately hoped would someday win the battle i wasn't sure you were even trying to wage.

we drank in the sun all day as you rolled yourself cigarette after cigarette and i breathed in your smoke and eventually we made our way to victoria park with our friends, to the same festival the rest of us had gone to the summer before. the one you'd missed out on last time because you'd been too skint to buy a ticket although you'd never been too skint to keep yourself drunk and high for days on end.

because old habits die hard and with old friends they resurrect, and because hypocrisy is a hallmark of denial, we all spent the afternoon doing more drugs than any of us had any business doing and we were so fuckeyed we wound up locked in the park after the festival had ended. we jumped the fence near the people's park tavern and the memory hardly serves but i do believe they served us more pints, although that was the last thing any of us needed. but that's how it always was with us. steaming and blind and somehow finding ourselves having just one more.

ensuring we'd numbed our senses so much that we'd drowned out any chance of feeling.

when there was nowhere left to go but home, you came back with me. back to the same house we'd lived in, just a year before. the one we'd both long since moved out of, but had not fully moved on from. the same house that held all the smoke and mirrors of our time together. the one between the flower market and the drug addicts. the one with your tiny room down the hall. the one still filled with our ghosts.

i was staying in our old flatmates room while she was away and somehow the two of us squeezed into her twin bed against the window at lord-knows-what-o'clock and in the subsequent daylight we lived out the same scene we'd performed in that house for half a year.

you felt hollow and vacant and familiar and alien all at once, but that was nothing new. but after half a month with someone who was so entirely different from you, it was harder than ever to pretend. even in a comedown. even in that house. even as we played out our script.

as you left i felt you leave. felt nothing and everything and wondered how even the best version of you could still leave me sitting in electrified indifference. how even living out a day with you that i had once craved could end with a morning that felt so cavernously void.

and here, reliving this now, i suppose i lied.

i suppose i do remember much more from our time together than i let myself believe. but perhaps the seeming holes in my memory serve more as guardrails than vacancies. perhaps the place i always held you served more as protection than indifference.

perhaps the walls i'd had up since the day we met served more as shields against a darkness i knew could consume me, than as apathy to how much i cared.

2010

2011

2012

2013

2014

2015

2016

i

august 2015 – 2016

and for quite a while after that

melbourne

for you, who taught me what insanity is

august – november 2015

melbourne

i find excuses to go to the pub and you find reasons to let me. you bring me bagels from the shop near your house and it feels like you've written me a sonnet that would make shakespeare himself weep. for a month we move closer than two separate entities could ever hope to be and all the while we hold the fusion at bay.

you are taken you are taken you are taken and we
    are not those people.

i
    am not that person.

and in retrospect it's easy to say perhaps you always were but in retrospect it's clear to confess that i had been that person before too.
but never like this.

no, never like this.

you leave the country to go and travel with her for a month and because i am good i do not contact you and because i am lewd i hope the relationship will not survive your journey.

and the relationship only survives the journey in that it would have been more of an inconvenience to you had you left her in bolivia when you couldn't really *leave her* in bolivia. and, how convenient for you, your messages to me begin again with mere days remaining before your flight home.

and, how convenient for you, you have me in waiting while she still shares your bed.

and, how convenient for me, it is all going exactly as my darkest hopes had planned.

the wheels hit the tarmac and my heart hits the sun and you come to lily blacks with everyone and i don't know if it's possible to contain the eternities trying to break free from us at once, but nothing has happened nothing has happened nothing has happened and so we drink simply the promise that it will. you tell everyone it's ending but what you don't say is what's beginning and i have never felt anticipatory joy the way i feel that night.

james and i go outside and he says he thinks you like me and he says it in the way only james can. with an understanding and a knowing and a love and a care that has never even dreamt of gossip or schadenfreude. he says it in the studied, sturdy way he delivers all his most poignant observations about the human condition. with a reverence and a grounded passion he himself is unaware he possesses. he says it like he knows it is secret. he says it like he knows it is truth. he says it like he is giving me permission to let myself fully fall.

and fall and fall and fall i did, with a force so strong it only felt safe knowing you would be there to catch me. but right at the moment my heart broke the sound barrier you built around your heart the most sound barrier and darling all that broke was me as you turned from *marry her* to *bury her*.

how do you mourn a promise? we were nothing we had nothing you gave me nothing and it was the most i had ever known. and when nothing was taken away it left dark matter where our life should have been and it took me years to heal the nothing you did to me.

maybe there was grace in it after all. if surviving *nothing* from you almost killed me then surely *something* would have taken me in this lifetime and all the rest. sent my soul back to oblivion, never to try my hand at being human again.

and maybe it was just more convenient for you. not to risk the same fate for yourself that you inflicted on me.

and maybe you were a coward and maybe you were afraid and maybe i was crazy and maybe none of it was real after all and maybe it was all more real than memory could even allow me to safely envision.

and look at me, ten years later, throwing out *maybe* as though you had never confessed. drunkenly, years down the line. that the universe our *nothing* had opened for you terrified you so much you chose instead to let me burn rather than risk igniting our bay-kept fusion in an inferno that would have consumed the sun.

22 november 2015

st. kilda east, melbourne

you invited me to the dinner that only your real friends were invited to, and i don't know if i had ever felt more excited to be part of something. me and you and them and the inside jokes i'd stood on the outside of for months. we talked about vegetables and the seasons when they grow and you knew the answer to every question because you know the answer to *every* question. an unparalleled encyclopedic mind that could get to the bottom of anything as long as it dwelled outside your own heart.

the others dwindled out the door that night and i stayed, under the guise of waiting for a ride that everyone knew i had no plans to call. being alone in your presence was more intoxicating than any of the wine we'd stolen from the pub. you'd rented a movie i'd referenced weeks before from the only rental store left in melbourne and you put it on for me and even though we didn't watch a single second of it, my heart lurched for how you listened and absorbed every piece of me so effortlessly. we talked in the way i knew we would talk and in that evening i saw futures unfurl before us.

futures you were entirely unbound to.

that night i slept in your bed dwarfed beside your body, and our lips never even touched. you, still beholden to another, if only by lack of the conversation we all knew was coming. me, beholden by some thread of moral code that had allowed me to invent reasons to see you and message you and think of you and yes even sleep in your bed but that prevented me from touching your skin until that conversation had been had.

how so much hinged on that conversation being had.

when the next day came i looked at my face in the morning light in the mirror of your bathroom and envisioned years of my face in the morning light in that mirror in your bathroom.

but i never saw my face in that mirror again. never stepped foot inside your home again.

you, who pulled me in so closely, only to barricade yourself away the moment the reality of heaven became tangible.

31 december 2015 – 1 january 2016
brunswick // fitzroy, melbourne

i bought a special dress for new year's and i had never done that before. had never put a new beginning on a pedestal as high as my hopes were for that night.

and i had put so many new beginnings on pedestals.

when midnight came you were nowhere to be found and when midnight came i was pacing around and when midnight came i finally saw you with your tongue down our coworker's throat. and my universe shattered and my dress felt idiotic and i don't even know if my eyes stayed dry long enough to get out the room.

they say how you start a year is how you spend it and 2016 started in shambles. the friend i'd known for a year and the friend i'd known for a month bringing me home in a heap, the former knowing a fragment of the story, the latter wondering what the fuck had happened to bring me from cloud nine to catastrophic heaves in the space of minutes.

my roommates were home already. blissfully drunk after they'd left whatever loft party they'd been at that hadn't quite suited them either. even after the wreckage of the bell toll, the shift in scenery was enough to give the night a second wind. through a haze of alcohol and heartbreak, we found ourselves playing and laughing and just being the kids we were, then. music blaring, doritos crushed into carpet, strangers becoming friends. ushering in a new era with the hope of being carefree.

when daylight came there were bodies strewn about the living room, as there so often were in that most magic of homes. maybe we were still drunk or maybe we were just alive with the current of being twenty-four, but we had one of those mornings you can only have when no one is trying. when nothing is planned. when everyone's nights went a little sideways and somehow the mayhem finds you all dancing in a living room until you really do just drop right where you stand. when waking brings laughter and joy and everyone piling into andy's twin bed to relive the debauchery of the night before, all while unknowingly living out another scene that will stay with you forever.

i

4 january 2016
st. kilda west, melbourne

we meet up on the beach in a part of town neither of us ever comes to. i take a bus there because the tram isn't running and we joke that i've lived here for a year and never taken a bus before. we sit in the sand to *talk* and before the first words come out i feel stupid for even wanting to meet you. you look at me with the pitying indifference i've grown terrified of seeing on your face and i know you're only here because you hoped placating me might end it all.

and i know you're only here because some part of you

still sees

the places in me

you once yearned for.

it felt like a cliche, even then. going to bali to try to figure out what the fuck was going on and just be alone with myself and this heart of mine that was trying to claw itself out from under my ribcage. to be on an island a world away, trying to gain the clarity on you i so desperately needed.

but that's where i'd found myself.

wandering rice paddies and eating smoothie bowls and talking to a girl whose story so intimately mirrored my own. overhearing hostel conversations between someday-influencers about vipassana meditations and how yoga had saved them.

your energy permeated everything. but in the distance from the life i'd been living for the last year and the torment i'd been in for the last month, i began to feel microcosms of truth.

i began to understand you were gone, even though your beguiling cruelty and your untold desire for me would still cast lines of hope my way for years to come.

i began to see the life i was destined for, the one with dusty feet and an untethered heart.

i began to feel the future i had always known, the one that called me with the gentlest voice, whispering across time:

you will live this.
you will survive this.
you will finally
find your way
> *home.*

i

summer 2016
bourke st, melbourne

the smell of sun-warmed sweat in clothes. stale. sweet. summer skin melting off into fabric. the smell of a body hard at work. that smell you know you aren't supposed to like but softly inhale as it wafts by. that smell will forever be you. since we spent the summer working in that cave together. watching you sling kegs, wanting nothing more than to be enveloped in that smell.

your body so close to mine for days on end.

but never touching me.

since strangers used to come in and assume we were together because even strangers could see the way you looked at me and even strangers knew that coworkers don't look at coworkers like that. since you spent a month showing me heaven and an eternity pretending it never existed.

that summer i spent loving you.

that i spent hating you.

that i spent hating myself.

it's been almost ten years, and the smell still brings me back to that dingy little bar. to you and your black button downs and the dawns spent desperately praying you'd suggest breakfast and the sunrises spent walking home in shambles, starving for so much more than the shitty 24-hour greek food we hadn't shared.

15 february 2016

south yarra // bourke st, melbourne

the theme of the event was *lords and ladies* and i dressed up as michael flatley and no one got it.

my friends and i drank cider on the roof all night and i was finally feeling human again, after two months of going insane.

when the event finished, i suggested we venture through the city back up to the bar that we ended all of our nights in, the one i worked in with you. of the dozen or so of us there were, i happened to take an uber with the only person in our group i never really spent time with. and as fate would have it, the driver who picked us up happened to be one of the comedians who came into her pub sometimes. and as fate would have it, this friend and this comedian had a bit of a rapport established. and as fate would have it, they got to talking and i sat and listened and when the comedian uber driver saw where she was taking us she casually said *do you know that comedian, laura? she's dating the manager there.*

and in an eternal instant my entire world shattered once more. the beautiful comedian who'd been lingering at the bar after shows lately. the deepened vacancy in you i could not explain. the breadcrumbs you had continued tossing my way. the glances and grazes and late-night revelations that proved to me some part of you still wanted me desperately, even while holding yourself at an ever-growing distance. the dots all simultaneously connecting, bringing my heart crashing down in the back seat of this comedian's car while dressed as a riverdancer and clutching the giant mylar balloon of the letter *B* i'd stolen from the venue.

my reality was ending anew but i held my shit together long enough to silently absorb all the words this comedian uber driver said and to excruciatingly listen to the unknowing and bantersome replies of the friend i never really spent time with. how she knew you'd broken up with the last girlfriend after south america, how she'd heard there was someone new, but she didn't know who.

how sweet it was, for it to be laura.

when the car pulled up in front of our bar, i don't even know if i could utter the words *thank you* as i crawled out of the backseat, mylar *B* in hands. standing in front of the cave that we worked in, you behind the bar just meters away, i managed to breathe just deeply enough to tell the friend i never really spent time with that i was actually going to go home.

me, the girl who never shied away from another drink. me, who spent hundreds of hours in that cave both working and not working. me, who had suggested we go there in the first place. me, the one who never left the party early.

i needed to go home.

she tried to convince me otherwise in that playful way friends do, but each word beyond the first few i'd managed to get out felt more and more dangerous as i could feel the floodwaters building in my throat. i handed her the *B* and said i was sorry and i think the hysterics started the second i turned my body away from hers. convulsing the whole way home, drunkenly trying, once more, to make sense of everything i had just heard. everything i now knew.

the darkest comedy of truth, rippling through me.

the way you hadn't been human enough to even tell me.

the way the fates had swooped in, to make sure i knew.

the most agonizing realization, once again. that not only had i not been good enough for someone i so desperately yearned for to choose, but i hadn't even been worthy of the truth.

i

summer 2016
melbourne

there are moments you give me everything

but eons you give me nothing

and i spend my weeks praying

for the fleeting second

   you will look at me

   the way you used to

just one more

      time.

summer 2016

melbourne

i hated you for turning the city i loved

into a place inseparable

    from the memory of you.

a shadow of a most haunted ghost,

lingering over every laneway

    and cafe.

6 april 2016
rainbow hotel, fitzroy, melbourne

i invited you to the birthday dinner only my real friends were invited to, and somehow i still felt so excited to have you be part of something mine. me and you and them and my life that you'd stood on the outside of for months now.

i was leaving the country in a few weeks and after everything we hadn't been and everything we wouldn't be, it shouldn't have mattered, whether or not you came.

and yet it still really fucking mattered, whether or not you came.

and in the end, your body showed up.

but you were nowhere to be found.

and somehow that felt even worse than if you had just never even bothered to appear.

the rest of us laughed and told stories and mused on my year to come, and you sat there in a way that made it clear you, once again, were only here to placate me. that you couldn't wait to finish your steak so you could make an excuse about unexpectedly needing to go into work and vanish from my life once more.

even after a summer of nothing, my expectations for that night had once again been the size of you and the proportionate disappointment of all you weren't was so immense it left me entirely incapable of feeling.

so i started my twenty-fifth year pretending it was fine and thanking you for coming and saying i understood you leaving and trying to save face in front of every other friend who'd made the effort to be there with me.

and you left and retreated to the cave that chained you.

and i looked out at the year ahead. a year that would see my body leave, while my heart stayed shackled to an idea of all you might have been.

june 2016

queenstown, new zealand

you told me you wanted to come to new zealand and go on a road trip with me and i hated you for suggesting it when you knew you would never do it and i hated myself even more for knowing, even after all you'd put me through months before,

i still would have gotten in that fucking car with you.

17 march 2017

new york city

you told me you wanted to come to america and go on a road trip with me and i truly abhorred you for suggesting it when you knew you would never do it and i truly abhorred myself even more for knowing, even after all you'd put me through over a year before,

i *still* would have gotten in that fucking car with you.

from when i left – when i returned
everywhere

november 2018
bourke st, melbourne

for years i wouldn't hear from you for months, and just when i thought maybe i was free i'd get a message that would take the air out of my lungs. 5am your time. and we both knew where your sudden honesty and care was coming from. and we both pretended you always spoke to me this way. and you would apologize for being shit and i would tell you you weren't shit even though you absolutely were. but that was love as i knew it then. you would say maybe you'd come to america and even though i knew you were lying, still i would start to plan the trip. just in my mind. just in case. and i would ask you for things you could never give me in the hopes that maybe one day you'd change.

for years in your wake the bar was set at exactly your height and i could never understand how something so tall could feel like dirt.

and for years i didn't know if it was possible to survive you.

and for years i didn't know if i even wanted to.

and after years of distance i still wondered if seeing you again would change everything. if somehow your mere gaze would derail every piece of me the way it had for so long. terrified to fall back under your spell but knowing i would never truly be free until i stood in front of you again.

years of energy and emotion and wonder culminating in one exact moment where you appeared and were—somehow, miraculously—simply human. flesh and bone with eyes that could no longer pierce through me to my core. an invisible hand relinquishing its grasp on my heart. a weight the size of you lifting from my soul. the space that you occupied forever cleared. open, once again, to receive.

september 2023

melbourne

it's been eight years since i first walked into that bar
    and into the purgatory of you
and i'm still a year younger than you were
    when we spent all those months not being together.
i still reread our old messages, from time to time.
still wonder if it really could have been
    as big as i know it was.
still wonder how something that was so small, in the end,
    could have taken up so much space.
still wonder if you think about me,
    in the same way i think about you.
still wonder if that one time—just that one time—
    you confessed to all you'd felt
if you meant it the way it felt like you'd meant it.

*   The way you understood me was always a lot to comprehend.*
*   Or rather the way we understood each other.*
*   There was a level of both sincerity and risk*
*   that being closer to you required*
*   and I found it terrifying.*

still wonder if no one has ever really terrified you in the same way.
    in the way you terrified me.
i don't think terror, in the end, has a place in true love.
and terror, in the end, was what you gave me.

2010

2011

2012

2013

2014

2015

2016

12

24 september 2015 – 23 april 2016

but never really

at all

melbourne

for #12, who taught me that sometimes
when you can't have the one you want,
you'll fuck the exact antithesis of that person
to fill the void

twelve

24 september 2015 – 23 april 2016

melbourne

fucking you
    felt like revenge

for the fact

that he
    did not
        want me.

2010

2011

2012

2013

2014

2015

2016

13

21 june – 29 september 2016

queenstown, new zealand

for #13, who didn't really teach me much of anything,
but who kept me warm all winter.
and made really good food.

june – september 2016
queenstown, new zealand

i was better at darts than you,

and you were better at pool.

all we really did for three months was play games and keep score

without ever once playing games or keeping score.

we'd found the only bar in queenstown with a dart board, and we spent our nights in the back corner, drinking beer from glasses with handles and playing cutthroat cricket on repeat because it was the same game i'd played three nights a week for four years, back when my life revolved around drunk frat boys and dive bars on the other side of the world.

you didn't have much to talk about and honestly that was exactly what i'd needed, then.

just a glorified drinking buddy who was kind and a little bland and always down for a pint and always happy to welcome me into your bed.

you cooked incredible food and told mediocre jokes and were endlessly easy to spend endless hours with because the hours were filled with so little. and after a year and a man that had left me as a shell of who i'd once been, easy and full and completely void of depth was precisely what i needed, when i'd found myself lifeless and frozen in the middle of a winter i had not experienced in ages.

winter 2016

queenstown, new zealand

i spend my days hiking
    through middle earth.

we spend our nights throwing plastic-tipped darts
    in the back of the dive
    no one else
    would be caught dead in.

i listen to nora jones and chance the rapper and tame impala on repeat
    while i dream on swing sets.

surrounded by ancient snowcapped peaks
    and aquamarine waterways carved by millennia,
somehow nothing about this place
        feels permanent.

19 august 2016
lake wakatipu

i say *have you ever been in a car accident?* as we wind between mountain and glacial lake. i reach for his hand. a quarter of a year spent naked in his bed and yet this is a moment of tenderness we've never once shared.

as soon as my fingertips touch him, my heart recoils.

we were never meant
    for moments
    like this.

2010

2011

2012

2013

2014

2015

2016

14

22 august – 7 september 2016

new zealand

for #14, who taught me how to have fun again

22 – 31 august 2016
south island, new zealand

you were fun and easy and smart and playful and pensive and light and carefree and careful and observant and kind.

you let it all be exactly what it was a not a single iota less.

it was goofy and weird and i still tell the story of how nothing actually happened until we went on the road trip i'd invited my friend along on, too.

how i told him as we packed the trunk together that there was a good chance you and i would be hooking up the whole time. how i had nothing to base that on other than the fact that we had started looking at each other differently in the last day or two.

he'd groaned and laughed and said my name in his irish accent and i made the face i make that says *i'm kinda sorry but also not that sorry and also you know me and also okay yes i really am sorry but also this is kinda funny, right?* we were all going to be drinking every night of the trip anyway, but he really hit the whisky in a way that excused him from what you and i were doing in the top bunk of the campervan we'd nicknamed *gary.*

any other triumvirate could have made for a miserable time but somehow the three of us living in that van together really was just stupidly fun. you and me stealing away in the parking lot of the franz josef glacier and hooking up in a public toilet while a tonal version of burt bacharch's *what the world needs now* played over the dinkiest little speaker in the bathroom ceiling and just laughing and laughing and laughing so hard at the insanity of it all that i don't actually know if we could finish what we'd set out to do in there. the fact that my wrist was broken and encased in a giant rainbow tie-dye cast and we had to maneuver around it every time, which would have been difficult enough in a normal bed, let alone on a mattress in the roof of a van with a 20-inch clearance to the ceiling.

the way the three of us hiked up a mountain with backpacks full of nothing but beer and irn-bru and toilet paper and somehow forgot the snacks and it just became a bit that never ended. eating crisp sandwiches and waiting for the avocados i'd brought from home to ripen for days and days and days on end until all of them turned dark at once and we had a smorgasbord of overpriced fruit on store-brand bread.

skipping stones on turquoise, and golden bay at sundown. sand flies and pancake stacks and that cave in abel tasman. the way you'd stay silent for an hour, taking everything in, and in a single sentence prove you'd understood more than almost anyone i'd ever met.

i still think of you when i think of good rocks and i still think it would have been fun, had our timelines intersected just once more. in another part of the world, on another adventure.

one more time, just to play.

one more time, just you and me and the fun and the ease.

one more time, and maybe this time without anthony sleeping two feet below us.

2010
2011
2012
2013
2014
2015
2016

13

21 june – 29 september 2016

queenstown, new zealand

for #13, who didn't really teach me much of anything,
but who kept me warm all winter.
and made really good food.

3 september 2016

lake tekapo

we take acid and it doesn't work

camping next to a glacial lake
water impossibly turquoise

i fall in love with the earth regardless

want my entire life to be spent this way
want my entire life to be spent so many ways

we sleep in a tent
     side by side

i'd told you we needed to stop hooking up
     and, for the moment, we had
          however briefly the hiatus may have lasted

i didn't want to be here alone with you

but everyone else had bailed
because they didn't really believe
     we weren't fucking anymore

and so then there i was
     not tripping
in a tent with you

in a place impossibly perfect

talking about shit

that didn't fucking matter

at all

14 – 29 september 2016

queenstown, new zealand

the reprieve lasted long enough for me to drive around the south island with him but not long enough for me to leave the country and not long after i'd gotten back from that joy ride, there you and i were again. getting drunk and playing darts and having the same formulaic sex we'd been having since before i'd called it off so i could explore new terrain.

but when i was leaving in a few weeks, what did it matter?

for the first time in my life, i was leaving in a few weeks

and it really just didn't seem

to matter.

winter 2016
queenstown, new zealand

i lied.

you did teach me
how to sink a ball
in the pool hall.

and that has to count
for something.

2010

2011

2012

2013

2014

2015

2016

15

20 – 29 september 2016
 and between. and since.

queenstown, new zealand

for #15, who taught me there might be hope
 for american men

an hour after we get to the bar i look over at you from the western saddle i'm straddling and say *do you want to go home and fuck* and in your slight georgia drawl you say *darlin i thought you'd never ask* and you grab my hand and we go home and get the whole thing right.

half a year spent sharing a bedroom and we never once touched until the night after i moved out. half a year spent in the second half of our twenties, sleeping two feet away from you and whoever you'd brought home that night while our friends in the states got engaged and got serious and thought about *settling down*.

in a winter that was so many things, you really were one of the best of them.

somehow always right there, but never with each other. sharing a bedroom, but never a bed. sharing a storyline, but never a story.

and in a lifetime that has been so many things, you really are one of the best of them.

somehow never right here, but always with each other. sharing beds, but never a bedroom. sharing our stories, but never a life.

2010
2011
2012
2013
2014
2015
2016
2017

16

30 april 2017

brooklyn

for #16, who taught me what cocaine feels like

sixteen

30 april 2017
bushwick, brooklyn

your best friend was so much more fun than you.

2010

2011

2012

2013

2014

2015

2016

2017

15

20 – 29 september 2016

8 – 15 june 2017

and between. and since.

queenstown, new zealand

williamsburg, brooklyn

for #15, who taught me there might be hope

for american men

fifteen

8 – 15 june 2017

williamsburg, brooklyn

you left oceania for the first time in years and came straight to see me in brooklyn, skipping right over georgia and your parents who hadn't seen you since you'd flown the coop forever ago. we got to the bar so early the morning you landed, the barista had to google how to make old fashioneds because she'd never made a cocktail before. we were shitfaced by noon and had sex on my roof overlooking all of manhattan and i'm sure all of manhattan was looking us over, too.

our old housemate came down from upstate to spend a few days with us and suddenly there we all were, the americans who'd left and returned. three friends who'd tasted life beyond the borders of the country that had tried to raise them in its image. three vagabonds strolling the highline together, sharing these wild hearts that could not be confined to the path that had been laid out.

we still laugh about the night we did so much molly my face went sideways. how i turned down a threesome with you and our friend, which really summed me up pretty well, honestly. no matter how fucked up life was, i still knew what i wanted. no matter how far from the earth i'd floated, i still knew what i didn't. no matter how sideways it all felt, somehow i'd still find my next foot forward on the trail i couldn't even see.

2010

2011

2012

2013

2014

2015

2016

2017

12

24 september 2015 – 23 april 2016
23 october 2017
but never really
at all

melbourne
manchester

for #12, who taught me that sometimes
when you can't have the one you want,
you'll fuck the exact antithesis of that person
to fill the void

23 october 2017

manchester

it had only been a year and a half since i'd seen you and somehow not a single cell of reality seemed to remain from the life i'd lived the last time we'd been in the same room. when i got so drunk at my going away that i cried when you refused to have sex with me and i made a scene in front of all of our friends who had had no idea we'd been stealing away after bar close to hate-fuck other people through one another's bodies for the last seven months. back when you were fucking me because i wasn't her and i was fucking you because you weren't him either. you were in love with her and i was in something with him and neither of us was remotely close to being anything like the people we weren't and it was kind of a perfectly aligned and dreadfully depressing friendship the two of us shared at the time.

but now, here we were. eighteen months to the day from that last night. ten thousand, five hundred, and forty-four miles away from where we'd last stood. in a tiny hotel room on dale street in a city i'd never been to before.

the time-distance between us had seen me live an entire life in queenstown: a dream job and broken bones and glacial lakes and mountain peaks and a few actual lovers and one man who'd simply filled space similarly to how you had. the unexpected move back to america: my sister's wedding just days after the world ended in early november 2016. how i'd stayed stateside and skipped the summer back in new zealand to try to *help* even though i was too paralyzed by the starting apocalypse at the time to know how to *help*. the three months spent aimless in chicago before the last-minute decision to move to brooklyn next week, and the six months spent there, unknowingly working for the mafia and entrenching myself in the craft beer world and doing my job like it was cocaine and cocaine like it was my job.

the inexplicable pull back to chicago in july, one i had never felt before in my life. a voice inside simply imploring: *leave new york. go home. you must go home.*

and my father's leukemia diagnosis just weeks later, suddenly the clarity on why i needed to be back there hitting me with the force that only the word *cancer* can wield.

the way my reality had turned from carefree escapades to every moment of free time spent in the cancer ward, terrified of the outcome that may await us. the way my life and my heart were somehow continuing on, even when it felt time herself had frozen and all feeling had calcified.

the man i had met, just weeks before you and i stood in front of one another in that hotel room. the one who i had known in an instant would change it all.

the one whose flesh i had not yet felt.

the one who pulled me so strongly, that in some convoluted way, i needed to touch you again before i let him touch me. some voice telling me that after my heart and my body had known his, there may never come another again.

and so here we still were. in that hotel room on dale street. having sex for what felt like might be the last time.

you, this man who always stood in place of the men i truly wanted.

you, who were ragged in all the right places.

you, who still managed to love me, even when both of our hearts were breaking.

2010

2011

2012

2013

2014

2015

2016

2017

8

31 december 2013 – 27 june 2014

6 june 2015

24 october 2017

london

manchester

for #8, who taught me how to come.

and who also

taught me

how to go.

2 april 2023
arambol, goa, india

i dream we're doing lines in the back of a taxi and even in the dream it feels wrong but i'm flying and it feels right. when i wake up my body is in india but my mind is in manchester and i wonder if you still do lines in bleak pubs, chasing some high you haven't felt since you were a teenager first doing lines in bleak pubs. i wonder if the darkness in you has seen the light of day. i wonder if you know the last time i saw you was one of the hardest nights of my life. both of us crying, trying to reach each other through a maddening cloud of alcohol and cocaine. our entire fragmented existence together, trying to reach you through an impenetrable haze of drug-fueled-drunken-fucking-turned-unbridled-chaos of the things never said and never known because you could never speak truth unless you knew you wouldn't remember it. and you remember everything. after years apart i'd hoped you'd changed but the second i saw you that night i knew you hadn't. pint after pint, line after line. you tried to lean on me but i was drowning in my own world too much then to bring you up for air and together we sank. in the morning i tried to talk to you about it but you pretended nothing had happened like you always did and i knew in that moment i would never see you again. i knew in that moment that i could never be the person you needed me to be, and you would never be the person i wanted. i knew you would never let yourself be reached and i knew for the life of me i could never again try. so without a word i took the train back to the peak district, back to lightness and safety and men who didn't make me wonder.

all i've ever hoped for you is that you let yourself be happy. and all i've ever prayed is that you let light in. and i still carry so much love for you, even if i'll never see you again. and sometimes, somehow, on mornings ten lifetimes away from you and us, i find myself wondering if you're still spending your days running from yourself in the same bleak pubs you've been running in for decades.

24 october 2017

manchester

that night you told me your mother asked for you on her deathbed and you didn't go to her.

i think you wanted me to finally hate you and even in that darkest of confessions, all i felt was heartbreak. for her, for you. for how much pain your pain continued to cause.

you were shaking like a ghost and i knew it was from all that you felt and do you have any idea how insane it is, that the only time you could feel anything was when you were drunk and coked out of your mind at three o'clock in the morning in the dingiest fucking hotel in manchester?

do you have any idea how much i understand how sane it is, that the only time you could feel anything was when you were drunk and coked out of your mind at three o'clock in the morning in the dingiest fucking hotel in manchester.

i know you feel so much you can't feel, and i know it's so overwhelming you'd rather die, and i know that heart of yours carries more in it than you'll ever let yourself acknowledge, and i know the fear of feeling even an atom of it is why you run and run and try to hide.

i know you'd rather be hated than risk being loved.

and i know you're fucking good at ruining things and i know it feels so fucked there's no hope to try and i know it feels like shining a light at all you feel will kill you.

i know, because our hearts have always been the same.

i know, because i was you.

but i know there is a pathway out, if you're ever brave enough to climb.

i know, because i've chosen the death we both avoided.

i know, because i have learned to feel it

and somehow

survive it.

eight

14 november 2023

melbourne

and all these years later, sometimes i find myself walking through a cloud of smoke and memory. a stranger on the street, smoking the same tobacco you used to fill our dingy little kitchen with. night after night. door cracked open to pretend we were clearing the air.

but we never cleared the air.

the weight and density of all we breathed out hanging heavy around us.

the whispers of soul never said aloud.

drifting over our senses, an impenetrable haze of poison disguised as oxygen.

how i loved
    breathing it all in.

eight

25 december 2023

suburbs, chicago

you send me a message saying merry christmas and it's 3am in england and i'm frozen in my tracks. ten years later and your words still freeze me. i haven't responded to anyone for days and yet somehow i know in the morning i'll respond to you saying *i hope you're well* and *sending love* and i do hope you're well and i do send love but i know you're not and i know you won't believe it. ten years since i walked in that flat and locked eyes with you. ten years since the new years party where we found each other on the roof. ten years since we said it would only happen once, and we'd never talk about it again.

ten years since you somehow loved me so deeply and touched me in ways no one had ever taken the care to touch me in before. ten years since we would stay up late drinking more than either of us had any right to and quoting movies back and forth and me trying to check in with you to make sure we were on the same page and you refusing to talk about anything that came within a lightyear of your heart. ten years since you turned ice cold and left me heaving my confusion out in silent wails.

ten years since maybe i was the one

who was made of ice

first.

2010

2011

2012

2013

2014

2015

2016

2017

2018

2019

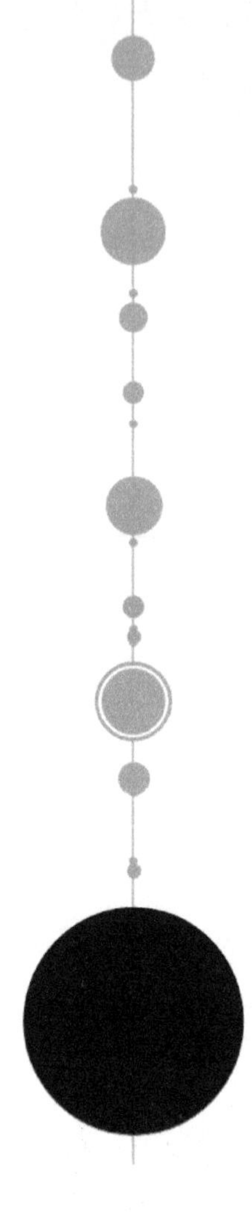

17

october 2017 – october 2018

march 2019 – august 2019

   and for lifetimes after that

chicago

earth

   for #17, who taught me everything

it doesn't seem fair, that most everything i've written about you chronicles the fallout, the grief. the hollow aftermath of trying to piece myself back together in the wake of the most immense joy i had known to that point.

it doesn't seem fair, to keep from the world the magic and moments that built the tower so tall that its collapse left wreckage for years.

but i was too enamored in the moments that built, to immortalize.

and too immobilized in their shadow to bring them to light.

this may be true of any human
    who has ever loved anything
        or anyone
but i truly do not believe
another living being has ever actually felt
    what it is i felt
when we were together.

the secret conversations
    in glances over the bar;
the way you simply standing
    in the same room
    could electrify the current
    running through my bones.

the way your departure
made each atom in me
divide itself in two.
and the way i felt
    every
    single
    split
    a trillion times
      over.

16 april – 1 october 2018

chicago

you began to sow our ending about six months after our beginning took root.

after i'd come home from a week in colombia where i'd spent my twenty-seventh birthday off grid in the jungle at a place i'd had to dirtbike up a mountain for two hours to get to and it was the most at ease and alive i'd felt in a year.

and you'd come home from a week in costa rica where you'd spent my twenty-seventh birthday in the rain forest at a place you'd had to take a seven hour bus and a two hour boat ride to get to and it was the most out of your element and alive you'd felt in your life.

and while i'd been away all i could think about was how much i loved you and how terrified i was of my dad dying.

and while you'd been away all you could think about was how much you loved me and how terrified you were of my love for you dying.

we sat at your kitchen table, in that early morning april light that can only glow on chicago days where it's still so cold outside, but the sun is fighting to bring life back to us all. soft, stretching sunbeams illuminating the hardwood and the fears you were finally ready to express.

i'd had a backpacking trip through asia planned since before we had met. set to depart that coming autumn, six months from the moment we were now sitting in at that table. a trip you had been invited on, almost immediately. a trip i had wanted, so desperately, for you to accompany me on. a trip i hoped would open both of our horizons to a life beyond our wildest dreams.

a trip, i had prayed, your solo week in costa rica would have given you the first taste of.

but instead, sitting at that table together—after you'd just traversed foreign soil alone for the first time in your thirty-four and a half years and told me how it had liberated you and changed you in unimaginable ways—you told me that you just didn't see how a future together was possible. i, this wildling who needed to roam free. you... you. this other thing. this other thing that you believed you were but i knew you did not have to be, if only you would choose to extricate yourself and come fly with me.

if only you would choose the you you'd tasted, just days before.

the you who had been bold enough to find himself in the most remote reaches of a foreign land.

the you who i knew had called to you your entire life.

the you who allowed himself to be truly free.

nothing to do with the actual act of traveling, and everything to do with the act of trust in a path you could not see.

but in that conversation, you chose your cage and to self-fulfil the prophecy you so feared, and my heart was so shattered i did not know how to begin trying to pry open the bars and change our stars.

you spoke while i absorbed, saying things like *you don't want kids and maybe i do* and *i just don't see how it's possible* and *you'll wake up someday and realize.* by logic your words made sense and by heart i knew they were lunacy. the version of me who existed then struggled to use her voice even in the simplest of moments let alone the most devastating. so there i sat in silence, listening to you seal our fate. all the while my head and my heart were screaming *you are wrong you are wrong you are wrong we can fight for this.*

but how do you begin to argue, when the person who is meant to be holding your heart in warmest safety now hands it back to you, hardly beating?

and so you made our decision. come october when my flight departed, our timeline would come to an end.

i would go. and you would stay.

half a year away.

half a year to spend in love and in turmoil, awaiting the execution date.

as far out from the end of it as we were from the start.

we repeated that kitchen table conversation infinite times between the first and the last. each time, my quietest voice trying to say *this is a mistake. we do not have to do this.*

come with me.

allow yourself to come with me.

but your fears were too grand and your mind too stubborn and each time you looked at me with torture in your eyes and said *i just do not see how we can make it* a layer of calcified protection grew around my heart.

six months spent begging you to keep me, while simultaneously preparing myself to live as the person you had discarded.

six months spent imploring you to join me in forever, while simultaneously accepting i would journey on alone.

i don't know how we could stand it, looking back.

so in love and so in pain and so unsure and still laughing and smiling and living a life that seemed normal,

even though nothing about the life we shared was ever normal.

madonna // whore

you had never met anyone like me and that terrified you.
how could i love you so deeply and hold you so closely
and nurture you so tenderly

    and still

    fuck you

    so carnally?

you punished me for the things you loved about me
because you couldn't stand the thought that other men

    had come

    before you.

you punished yourself for the things you loved about me
because you couldn't stand the thought of punishing me

    for the men

    who had come

    before you.

but how could i have become everything you loved
without every single one

    of the moments

    that lead

    to you?

the other heads crying in my lap
the other hearts borne open to me
the other savage love affairs that allowed me

    to tear down my walls

and become wild

    again.

2 august 2018
janesville, wi

we take the back roads for the joy of it, windows down the entire way
and you make it seem like you've been waiting your whole life
just for someone to say taking the scenic route is okay.

we spend the night in janesville
and fuck on the roof of a parking garage
and take a bath in a jacuzzi tub
in a victorian house we say we'll buy someday.

that night you cry while holding me
under that canopy of a four-poster bed.

we feel safer with each other than we've ever felt,
but it's a safety you're convinced can't last
        because i've always been terrified of safety.

and lord knows, you were right.
but lord knows, we didn't want to see it.
and lord knows, it almost killed me.
but lord knows, i am so grateful
        you let me

                go.

2018

chicago

he always acted
like he'd caught lightning
    with me.

like he was just waiting
for the moment
i electrocuted us all
    with my
    very nature.

i went to the weddings
    of former lovers

    and it drove you mad.

that i could hold their brides
    in my heart
    and in my arms
and that they could love me.

that i had been held by these men
    in their hearts
    and in their arms
and that they continued to love me.

would you have rather
    that every man
    who had loved this body,
    this vessel of mine,
    had cast my heart aside,
    left me for dead?

but you, try as you might,
    could never
    extricate love
        from flesh.

september 2018

chicago

you were plagued

by the paralyzing notion

    that all you were to me

    was another number

        in the pages

        of my history book.

isn't it agony,

    how our prophecies

        fulfill

           themselves?

12 – 17 september 2018

san juan island // vancouver island

half a month before i was set to depart we decided to take a trip to the pacific northwest in some kind of bittersweet attempt to squeeze joy out of the thing we were slaughtering. i'd suggested hitchhiking through iceland and we compromised on renting a car and taking a ferry to canada.

we planned the first few days around a *minus the bear* song we'd both loved, and you acted like the mere idea that we could find ourselves somewhere beautiful simply because we'd followed a melody there was the most revolutionary feat two humans had ever accomplished. but to me this was the only way that had ever been worth living. we drank coffee in a treetop rope fort and hiked along idyllic coastline and i guided us to roche harbor to take in the haze of lights and drink a bottle of red wine.

when we'd lived out our song, we ferried to vancouver island and drove to the sleepiest little oceanside town to spend a few nights living in a treehouse and hiking through redwoods. you declared repeatedly the whole time we were away that you wanted to live out here, that people just live out here, that you could live out here and i said *yes yes yes* and i so desperately wished that you would actually allow yourself to follow that call. to follow something in your heart that spoke to you beyond the confines of the life you'd convinced yourself you needed to live, even if it meant living it without me.

as we made our way back to the treehouse one of those nights, we started talking about my trip. about the adventure i was set to depart on in two weeks time, the adventure you had chosen not to accompany me on because it did not fit into the path you had decided you needed to make yourself walk. i told you my plans for the first month, including seeing one of my best friends and his girlfriend in the city they now lived in.

at the mention of a man—a man i had known and loved for almost a decade, a man i was going to visit *with his girlfriend,* a man who *even if i had wanted to fuck i would have been free to because you had made the decision that we were not going to be together once i got on that flight to the philippines—* your entire demeanor changed. as it always did when, over the course of the last year, i had made mention of any man who was not you.

and somehow there we were, two weeks away from me leaving and none of this mattering, sitting in a car in front of this treehouse. me, trying to placate your anxieties over this friend of mine who had never once been a threat to you. just as i had done a thousand times before with any number of my friends who had never once been a threat to you.

as the conversation dragged on and i exasperatedly explained, once more, my ability to simply *love people* and let them love me regardless of gender or sex or the physicality that may or may not have ever been involved, something in my brain switched. i had held this anxiety for you for almost a year and i had held it with love and understanding and i knew you didn't want to feel the way you felt and for so long i had been willing to have this conversation on repeat. but in an instant an irreversible awareness shifted and suddenly a year of my repeated explanations not having changed an iota of your trust in me or understanding of me turned my compassion into absolute fury.

i said the words *i can't have this conversation with you anymore* and i said it in a way you knew, instantly, i meant i was *done.*

it's crazy, how the energy of an evening can change in a second. how the energy of an entire relationship can change in a second. after a year of me on the defensive, now you were the one sitting there trying to explain something unexplainable. how you hadn't really meant some component of all you'd feared. trying to walk back the jealousy and shame you had thrown all over me.

but the light had been turned on, the clarity gained.

and even if it would take years to fully reconcile, in that moment i began to reclaim a part of me you had unknowingly been stripping bare since the day we met.

16 september 2018

vancouver island

before i left you, we planned an escape together

knowing i was leaving

wanting to savor those last weeks.

on the beach on vancouver island

someone had written *will you marry me?* in the sand.

i joked and asked if it had been you.

would you say yes if it was? you'd replied

i told you no.

what i didn't say was

    how stupid a question.

    how idiotically narrowminded.

for if the question had been

    would you spend the rest of your days on this earth loving me

    and laughing with me

    and never growing up?

i would have screamed a thousand *yes*es into the sea.

but you were always so caught up on the semantics

and not the love

that was right in front of you.

16 september 2018

sooke, bc

sometimes when it rains,

 i think of being cooped up in that treehouse

    at the edge of the earth with you.

and i feel this really sad ball of joy glow inside of me.

and i wonder if maybe i should just sit down

    and watch the entire lord of the rings trilogy.

and i wonder if you ever think of that treehouse when it rains, too.

7 october 2018

the philippines

early october and i'm on an island a world away. palm trees and beaches and less than 170 square miles to cage me as i pace paradise trying to escape you. as i pace paradise not knowing if i ever can escape you. not knowing if i could ever even want to.

we schedule a call because we schedule these things now and we aren't together but we're still here for each other and frankly it's bullshit and frankly the only reason you aren't on this island with me is because you decided you couldn't be. part of me wants to hate you for that and more of me loves you so much i can't even see the vitriol that will someday come, however fleetingly.

you call with your voice because seeing my face would be too much and i sit in the sand and pretend i think we did the right thing and you tell me about how you know it's hard but it has to be this way and how you haven't been sleeping at all. you ask me how the island is and i don't remember what i say but the truth was that it was beautiful and the truth is that it was hell. and everywhere i go, there you are. there you are, because there you aren't. there you are, because you chose to stay in concrete rather than plunge into the sea with me and this place is meant to be heaven and it just feels like purgatory and there is so much i want to say to you but you made this choice for us and i grew too tired of trying to tell you you were wrong that i just shut down and now i sit in the reality you made for us and listen to you tell me you still love me but you know this is right somehow.

you ask if i've met anyone and we both pretend you mean friends and we both know you're petrified i've moved on already. what you don't mention is that you'll fill the hole my absence left in your heart with someone who could never be me. and i don't even ask because i don't even care and not in a way that i didn't care but in a way that i cared so much it really was just that whatever made you happy was all that mattered.

the call lasts two hours and half the time is just silence and hearing each other breathe and remembering when that breath was our life together. part of it feels pathetic and more of it feels like the only thing keeping me alive. while the line is active, i'm with you and while the line is active, you're in me and while the line is active, the morphine drip of your existence floods my veins enough to keep the torture of you not being with me and you not being in me at bay.

when we've said our goodbyes you tap end and the line goes dead and i would have sat there waiting for you to end it forever. would have sat there with you, never ending it, forever. but you cut the line off and suddenly i am back on my paradise hellscape alone in the dark with stray dogs and tree frogs and an inbox full of messages from people i don't want to talk to saying *it looks like you're living the dream.*

the truth is the only dream i'd had for the last year was that you would be here with me. and the truth was i was living a dream i wasn't sure i even wanted anymore. and the truth is that fulfilling my dreams would come somewhere in the middle, somehow. a future forever painted in the shades we'd made together. a life completely sown in the soil we'd tended. a world of my own making, crafted from the shards you'd left me in.

a mosaic covered in love, tinted in a hue only we could see.

i would have spent
a lifetime
throwing starfish
back into the sea
with you.

it would have mattered
to me.

24 october 2018

hanoi, vietnam

the streets were so busy they kept my mind off you

if only for the fraction of a second it took

    to avoid getting run over.

you

    moped

        you

semi

    you

    moped moped taxi   donkey cart

you   you   you

my friends took me to a cement slab in the sky where we could watch the sun set over the city.

    you would have loved it.

but you'd chosen to stay behind.

you'd chosen to let me leave.

you'd thought this time and space weren't for you.

who knows

maybe you were right

maybe you would have hated how congested it was and how the restaurants are really just peoples living rooms and how there are no traffic laws.

    okay.

you would've hated that there are no traffic laws.

but you would have loved it, too.

but you wouldn't allow yourself to even consider loving it.
just like you wouldn't allow yourself to even consider
    loving the wildest places
    that dwelled
    within me.

29 october 2018

ha giang, vietnam

this morning i motorcycled through a police barricade and rode to the top of a vietnamese mountain. i found a homestay in a rice paddy where i'll sleep next to a barn and as i watched the sun set over china i felt the tiniest flash of peace. the most fleeting glimpse of the future. a voice, a vision, that said *you will find your freedom.*

a trust in my heart, that vanished almost as quickly as the sun behind the rolling peaks, that promised i was on the right path.

that assured, despite the wretched heartache of our parting, that, somehow, this really was right.

that i was finally on my way

to where i knew

    i truly belonged.

december 2018

fitzroy, melbourne

she asks if i'm dating anyone and my stomach drops out at the mundanity of the question. at the timing of the question.

i don't *date*, i tell her. i never really understood it. certain souls have existed in times and spaces, yes. they came in when it was right. we parted when it was right. many have stayed as friends, i say.

i never sought them. they simply arrived.

what i don't say, was that then there was *you*.

what i don't say is that i can't even think about another hand touching my skin. what i don't yet know is that it will be almost a year before i allow another hand to touch my skin. what i don't yet know is that i will go back to you. but your hands will never again feel the same. what i can't yet know is that this will break my heart more than anything.

you should write a book someday, she tells me.
i'm sure i will, i reply.

my voice in front of her,
   my mind drifting
   ten thousand miles
      away.

6 december 2018 – 14 january 2019
fitzroy, melbourne

fourteen months after i had first invited you to come on this journey with me,

eight months after the kitchen table conversation where you'd declared our futures were incompatible and i first started trying, in vain, to tell you you were wrong,

two months after i'd left and we'd parted ways because it was what you had said needed to happen,

two weeks after i told you i was still grieving us, but had started tasting glimpses of the future in which we both were finally okay without one another, that i'd started to trust, ever so slightly, that maybe you'd been right,

on a december morning in the city and in the future that were meant to be cleansing you from me,

you called and said

i think we made a mistake.

and i'd be lying if i said it didn't make me a little mad, even now, thinking about the audacity you'd had.

and i'd be lying if i said it wasn't a little sad, even now, how scared you must have been, watching me start to fly free without you.

the conversation lasted hours and it got us nowhere except to send me reeling.

after six months of getting over you while still being with you and two months of moving past you while still talking to you, there you were. reopening the door you had slammed in our faces.

if i am entirely honest, as i so desperately hope to be, the deepest, truest, most aware piece of me knew, even then, that i could not go back. that the future in which we worked it all out had already slipped through our fingers. that the independent wildness in me you had so loved and so feared had taken root in a way that could never again be weeded out.

but every single other piece of me had waited for two thirds of a year to hear you say those words. and even if that deepest, truest voice knew it was too late, the yearning in me to go back to *the way it was* and the way we'd felt was so ardent that it clung to the hope you'd cast to the other side of the planet and allowed me to wonder if maybe i really could go back.

we spent december spiraling. dancing in circles around *what to do* and *what made sense* and suddenly my summer of freedom back in the city of my dreams was being overcast, once again, by a man who hadn't chosen me while he'd had me.

our broken record conversations got us nowhere and finally we decided to spend january not speaking to get some clarity and i decided to spend january in another country because i could not handle being back in this place now that the ghost of you was waiting for me down every laneway, too.

and so, once again, i left a place i loved because i could not think while i paced it.

and so, once again, i spent mid-january on another island after a love that festered through an australian december had driven me to madness.

and so, once again, i found myself entirely alone on foreign soil trying to figure out what the fuck was going on.

18 – 29 january 2019
anuradhapura, sri lanka

eight thousand eight hundred and eighty miles away from you—in the middle of the night in a monastery in rural sri lanka, cut off entirely from the world for a week—i knew you were dead.

knew, as certainly as i knew my own name, that something had fallen on your head at work and killed you.

doubled over atop a rusted, rickety cot, i sobbed uncontrollably. fear and grief coming from a depth of my body that i had rarely tapped into before. i cried in a way i hadn't in years, even through my father's leukemia and through the pain of losing you the first time. i cried so hard i was drowning. drowning in anguish. drowning in an endless onslaught of tears. drowning in my inability to fill my lungs between each bout of utterly overwhelming dismay at your departure from this life.

i wailed entirely in silence.

i'd first heard the word *vipassana* exactly three years to the day before my first meditation started—in bali, on the island i'd fled to from another melbourne december in an attempt to understand what was happening with a man who'd spent the month turning my mind to mayhem. and i didn't put that dot together for years. all i'd known this january was that somehow the only sane thing that seemed worth doing in the insanity i'd plunged into, was to spend ten days in silent, isolated meditation. ten days without speaking. ten days without reading, writing, listening to music. ten days where even eye contact with another living being was discouraged. ten days spent sitting on a thin pillow on the floor for eleven hours a day, surrounded by nothing but monks and the sounds of the sri lankan countryside.

just me. and my thoughts. and the hope that maybe, somehow, i could meditate myself to clarity on you. that maybe, somehow, i could meditate myself to liberation.

on the sixth night, the night i knew you had died, i grieved you entirely and i grieved you mutedly.

every fiber of my being wanted to leap off of the flimsy mattress i called my bed and run to one of the sleeping monks, to beg them in a language i didn't speak to let me have my phone back. i had never needed something more than to hear your voice in that moment, to know that your death was a fabrication of my solitarily confined, meditative mind.

but instead of waking the entire monastery, i sobbed inaudibly. alone.

i prayed to a god i didn't know if i believed in that this overwhelming feeling, this *knowledge* of your death was somehow made up. my soul implored me to take action, my mind knew, even if you were dead, there was nothing i could do about it from here. i had vowed upon starting this meditation to not break my silence, to deal with each emotion as it came, to give myself over fully to the power of the practice. it was a vow i had not taken lightly, but one i could not have appreciated the weight of until this moment.

so somehow i moved through it. soothed myself enough to breathe. and told myself—rules about *not talking to each other until february* be damned—that the moment i got my phone back in four days time, i would message you.

and i told myself that whatever the fuck this thing was i had opened in myself, i did not want it.

so for four more days, i simply sat on the floor. no meditation technique, no attempt to liberate myself. just sitting on the ground and thinking and counting the minutes until i would hear your voice again. until i would know you were alive. in some moments feeling, with shaking clarity, that if i could sense you that strongly a world away, i must be destined to return to you. in other moments knowing, with petrifying certainty, that the intensity of that connection was simply a testament to all that existed.

when the endless minutes finally passed and my phone was back in my hand, i turned it on ready to reach out you. after ten days off grid, a lit screen felt foreign in my palm, but as my eyes adjusted to the unnaturalness of the glow, there, clear as day, appeared a message from you.

sent four days prior, in the middle of the month in which we were not supposed to be speaking.

I know you don't have your phone on, and while I feel silly sending this out to the void, it just doesn't feel right to not tell you.

you had had an accident at work. something had fallen on your head. and of all the medical centers in chicago, they had taken you to one eight miles away from the brewery, to the same floor of the same hospital we had been in just ten months prior, when you'd sat with me as i donated stem cells to save my father's life.

you had sat mere feet away from where the ghosts of us still lingered, and i had felt you on the other side of the earth.

you were fine, the *CT scan says there's nothing to worry about.*

but it had been bad enough for a ct scan and stitches and a rush to the hospital. to that hospital.

it had been bad enough that, in a month of our mutually agreed upon separateness, you reached out to me. knowing i would not see the message. knowing i could not reply.

but i had known.

through time and space and cosmic connection, i had known.

as my eyes read your words, my heart collapsed in on herself in understanding and in love and in fear and in truth and in uncertainty and in conviction.

certain of the thread that bound us. unconvinced that you truly understood. terrified of all i had seen. knowing that something limitless had been tasted.

that there was an opening in myself that could never again close.

the moment i returned to you, i knew i had not come back.

i flew across the globe and surprised my sister for her birthday and after a night spent laughing on her sofa, i made my way to your doorstep for the first time in one hundred and forty-eight days. one hundred and forty-eight sunrises without you. one hundred and forty-eight eternal lifetimes alone.

when i came up the stairs and opened the door of your apartment for the reunion we had spoken of at length, you were hiding in your bedroom. you were hiding from me.

i stood between the entry and the foot of the sofa alone and watched as you slowly peered around the doorframe. as though you were scared i was real. as though you were afraid to even set your gaze upon me.

i think you thought it would be cute, somehow. or maybe you really were just so terrified of me that you needed to hide.

but in that moment, the second i saw you peeking like a scared little boy around that wooden frame, i knew.

i knew i had known since the instant you called me in december and i knew i had known even as i thought you were dead and i knew i knew then.

i had long grown on.

your fear of all i am was far too much for me to hold again.

your terror of all you knew i could be was never going to free me.

your refusal to meet me at my destined heights would chain us both.

but the truth of that knowledge still scared me so greatly that i pushed it away. even as i felt appalled by your awe of me and repelled by your touch, i told myself that this was just part of the process of coming back.

i convinced myself that the screaming in my body of *no no no* would yield in time, and give way to the ease we'd once known.

15 april 2019

andersonville, chicago

she's supposed to be one of my closest friends and when she and i sit at the same exact bar you and i spent our first night together at and i tell her i think maybe, somehow, i've stopped loving you the way i did before and nothing has ever terrified me more, all she says is that i'm lucky to have a good man and i should just be grateful for that. because *she* has never been so lucky.

what i'm trying to tell her is that it feels like my heart is attempting to extricate itself from my ribs and i don't know if i can survive even the idea of losing you again, let alone the reality of it. that it nearly killed me the first time but at least then it was a choice that was made and not my love for you betraying us. what i'm trying to tell her is that opening the door to even consider that that might be the truth of how i feel is making me have panic attacks weekly.

this love for you, that had once felt eternal as the stars in the sky. this love for you that i had felt extend from the moment we met until the day i died and never in a million lifetimes had it occurred to me that the day i died would come as a self-inflicted severing of you from my soul.

i lay this at her feet in honesty and in fear and she hears only what she wants to hear, and meets it with words that all but say,

> *suck it up and rot with him for eternity, because i am miserable, and i blame my misery on my being alone. and every man i let into my life treats me like a doormat and i let them and somehow because of that it means that you should stay in this thing that feels treacherously hollow, because being dead next to a good man is better than being alone.*

and her bitterness feels like a grapefruit rind to the heart.

and her selfishness leaves me further marooned on the island of my own making.

and her emphatic defense of you as *a good man* is the only thing about which i know she is absolutely right.

the night after that cubs game i took the bus right past your house and i didn't tell you i was going home because i needed to prove that i could. you said you'd hoped i'd come to you like i always did and i said i was tired but i really just needed to know i could still exercise my own autonomy.

a year spent going to you night after night after night and the reality was, for a year i'd wanted nothing more than to assume every day ended in a night coming for you.

but i had left, and then my body came back but my heart never did and now you wanted me in that bed again and somehow the arms that had always felt like safety now felt like a cage.

my whole body used to convulse for you and now it was revulsed by you and i had no idea what to do with that.

and so in indignation i left wrigley field and knew it was a lie of omission to not even mention to you that i was a block away but i didn't care because at least subversive defiance meant

i still had

free will.

20 may 2019

north center, chicago

31 july 2024

barbados

there was a time where it seemed inconceivable that a day would ever arrive when julia jacklin might come on shuffle and it wouldn't immediately make the floor of my stomach fall out. all those months, masochistically listening on repeat and heaving the weight of you out in guttural sobs.

but tonight, five years after that summer, she plays unexpectedly as thousands of songs cycle through and i feel, yes. i feel.

but i feel peace. i feel love. i feel solace.

i think of how you had found the album in a record shop in nashville. had played it for me when you got home. how your eyes had done that thing they do when you hear music that takes you to some other place; some other place music has never taken me in the same way. how we sat listening together on that same sofa where you'd held me after i had that panic attack at work when my dad was sick and i'd realized my blood was the thing that would either save him or kill him and they sent me home early because i couldn't breathe and you put on spongebob because you didn't know what else to do with the still shaking shell of me who'd arrived on your doorstep and how that was exactly the right thing to do, then. how back then, before you'd let me go, you always knew exactly the right thing to do.

how much that had changed.

how had that much changed?

there we were, fifteen months later, listening to the album that was poised to get me through tearing my soul away from yours for a second time.

you, introducing me to the very tonic that i would use to cleanse you from my life for good.

i wonder now, if you knew then. that her chords spoke to you in that record shop because we'd both need them. if in some way, you playing that record for me that may morning was an offering. a lifeline.

how that very next day you'd finally vocalized the thing you'd been terrified to bring to light for the three months since you'd had me back. had my body back, but not my heart. how my heart had stayed somewhere neither of us could find, but both of us were praying might return. almost as though julia had forced you across a mental rubicon and you couldn't hold it back any longer and you just needed to hear me say it.

how i couldn't even say it.

how hearing the words of the truth of my being come out of your mouth felt like purest liberation and the most crushing, excruciating pain. how i knew you were right; knew you were setting me free. for good this time.

and still, i would have bled my own veins dry if it meant not feeling the way i felt. if it meant you were wrong. if it meant i could still be in love with you, the way i had been before we let it all go.

but the truth was, your skin had changed. your touch had become foreign. and of all the pieces of you i had turned a blind eye to losing, your body as a home was the one i could not feign still remained. you'd felt me recoil from you; listened as my screams dwindled to sighs.

how we both pretended i'd always come for you like that.

how we both pretended i wasn't now coming in spite of you.

you laid the words at my feet, both of us knowing they were true. and—julia's face staring at us from the album cover propped against your record player—my chest caved in on itself and i didn't know if i would ever be able to stand again. laying naked on your couch, gasping for air between choked sobs. terrified to move. to leave that moment. to pick my body up off of those cushions. knowing that the second i left that sofa, we could never go back. the moment my bare feet touched the hard wood, it would really be over.

i would have stayed on that couch forever; would have stayed in that moment forever, if you'd have let me.

floating, naked, raw, real.

but you made the first move, like you always did. and the moment shattered. and we had to move on. and i had nothing left to do but stand up because without you on that couch next to me there was no reason for me to stay and in the instant you stood up i had never felt more alone. i had put clothes on in front of you a thousand times before but never like this. but somehow i did. and standing in front of you fully dressed was the most unnatural thing i'd ever known.

and i knew—after months of pretending i didn't; months of praying i didn't—that this was it.

knew we could never go back.

knew we would try, but only because this feeling felt worse than death herself and that both of us would scramble and grasp at anything to avoid the pain of this reality. to avoid the other having to face the pain of this reality.

how i would have spent a hundred years drowning at the bottom of the deepest ocean if it meant i could have spared you from any of it.

and for years it did feel like drowning at the bottom of the deepest ocean, entirely unable to die. for years i didn't know if i could ever truly be free. for years i wondered if i'd been wrong even though i knew i was right.

so for years when julia's voice would appear, my chest would tighten; my mind, derail.

so imagine my surprise, tonight. after all these years, somehow to find that her music can exist in a world in which my breathing does not change. my stomach does not lurch.

a world in which i simply sing the words, and the words, for the first time, have extricated themselves from you.

may 2019
chicago

the relief
felt
like a betrayal.

may 2019

north center, chicago

there were a thousand tiny moments in which i was afraid you were losing me, but only a handful where i realized i was already gone. i don't even remember the context; don't even remember the joke you tried to make. just remember you throwing it in my face, the way i'd broken my own bones as a child.

just remember you laughing and snidely saying something about me doing that again. just remember the look on your face the moment you saw the look on mine. just remember knowing you knew instantly that it had never even occurred to me you could be that cruel. knowing you knew instantly that you'd crossed a threshold you could not return from. knowing you knew instantly that i had entrusted to you the most delicate of secrets, and you had just shattered it before me, laughing.

the thing is, you did always know when you'd fucked up.

but you only knew through the pain you felt

through me.

june 2019
chicago

we sign up to get our motorcycle licenses and your friend who never liked me signs up too. it was a last-ditch effort to pretend something might be salvageable between us. that somehow us getting those licenses would mean you were actually going to bring the motorcycle that had been sitting in a garage in new jersey for five years out to chicago, like you'd been saying you were going to as long as i'd known you. that motorcycle, this invisible barometer for the freedom you refused to allow yourself to accept. sitting in that garage, unused. yearned for. talked about at length. and never attained.

in the months i was away—before we started pretending we could save things, back when you'd decided our futures weren't meant to intertwine— i'd motorcycled through the mountains of vietnam. unlicensed, unlearned. just a quick lesson from the hostel worker in a parking lot, and off into the mountains i went, dodging semis and washed-out roadways on cliffside highways hardly wider than an alley. all the while, actively allowing myself to grieve you. actively convincing myself it was better this way.

but now here i was. back on american concrete, trying to unconvince myself that the life i'd tasted in your stead had opened a truth in me that i knew could never again be sealed.

the idea of licensing freedom was more foreign to me than any country i'd been free in, but the desire in me to go back to *the way it was* was so immense i was blind to the cage i was trying to force myself to live in for you.

so i agreed to take the class and do things *the right way* and i felt panic in my fascia every time i thought of going to that parking lot with you and the friend who never liked me. my body screaming at me, as she had for months, that all of this was wrong. my mind refusing to hear her pleas, because the fear of the pain of going through it all again was greater than my fear of a life of suburban mediocrity had ever been.

and my fear of a life of suburban mediocrity was so immense it had driven my entire wild existence, up to the point of deciding to come back to you.

but two weeks before the class was set to start, the facade broke and you confessed how i felt for us both and i'm still not really sure how we did it, looking back. how we could watch it all falling apart at the seams once again, and still have conversations about things like whether or not i was going to take that class with you. how i was able to make a joke about your friend running me over if i even dared.

after all that, when the day finally came you went with the friend and they ended up turning you away because they didn't have a helmet that could fit you.

it's laughable, really. how the metaphors write themselves.

you, still trapped by your mind. still stuck in the thoughts that kept you from simply accepting the freedom you could see right in front of you. still waiting for some kind of guarantee of protection before you jumped into what it was your heart craved.

me, inching to the edge of how things were *supposed* to be, and incinerating it all when the whispers of my heart turned to screams i could no longer ignore.

2 july 2019
la higuera, chile

i shattered my own heart into a million pieces, and i've come on a last-minute journey to the chilean desert with one of my most eternal friends to sit in the totality of a solar eclipse in some kind of desperate cosmic effort to try to put myself back together.

my first experience in totality brought love.

maybe the second will bring it back.

we find a tiny town in the desert that feels as though it's never seen an outsider until thousands of us arrived for this one celestial moment. we set up camp on a hillside over a valley and soon begin kicking a ball around with our chilean neighbors.

my mind tells me to retreat from these people, to be alone, to let sadness consume me.

my heart tells me to trust the joy and connection that's in front of me.

i learned a long time ago which one knows best.

and, here and now, i am relearning to listen.

the night before the eclipse we sit around a fire with our new friends. they sing songs and tell stories and we pass bottles of wine between us.

my spanish is good enough to listen, but not good enough to speak.

it is exactly what i need.

i eventually leave the fire and lay under the stars. i ask the cosmos for guidance and feel nothing but the wind whipping gently by.

it's winter here, but blistering summer in chicago. in the city where i've left you. how quickly warmth turns to cold and back again when we let it.

we spend the next day watching the sun and moon chase each other across the sky, eagerly awaiting the moment to come.

the earth grows darker as the sun becomes more and more obscured, and i feel myself grow heavier and lighter at the same time. electricity coursing through me, anticipating the moment i hope will bring the clarity i haven't been able to grant myself.

when totality finally comes, involuntary shouts of pure jubilation rise up through the desert valley.

i feel a rush and release and a return to myself and a love for this planet all at once.

i cry and laugh and sigh and say *thank you.*

i scour the heavens as though in this moment of pure godly magic they will show me my exact path. that they will tell me what to do. that the stars will align and spell out the words i've been waiting to see.

all i hear is *you know what's true.*

and i do.

and i don't.

and i'm terrified.

and the world spins on.

and light returns to the day.

i never understood homesickness
until i met you

6 july 2019
belmont harbor, chicago

you asked me questions
    you couldn't handle
    knowing the answers to
and then punished me
    for telling you
    the truth.

26 july 2019
addison st, chicago

i wear my pure white sundress when we meet up

and if i'm honest on some sick level it's intentional

because if i'm honest on some sick level

i want to hurt you

    for hurting me.

and if i'm honest we both know

    i never would have been your bride.

but i would have spent forever

    loving you.

and if i'm honest i want you to see me

in this white dress

and remember

    that it was you

    who let me go

    the first time.

and i have never intentionally hurt you

and i am so sorry

    for wearing this dress.

but if this dress is the only time through all of it

that i try to put salt in the wound

then by god

    maybe we really did

    do right by each other

        after all.

you tried to keep me
in all of the cages
you'd built in your own mind.

but darling we both always knew
    someday
my wings
    would have to break free.

separating myself from you felt like
separating my soul from my body.
i didn't know where you began
    and i ended.

how do you extricate two things
that cannot exist
without each other?

august 2019
chicago

i had gotten to keep
everyone
i wanted to keep
before you.

8 september 2019

north center, chicago

the day we sat on your roof for the first time was also the last time. and we both knew it. through tears, you told me you were so grateful for me. you told me i would meet someone else someday. and i was so mad at you. how quick you were to write yourself off. how quick you'd always been to write yourself off. how you'd always believed my love could be given so freely.

i didn't say it then, but i knew you were wrong. you were the one of us who always threw yourself into the next person. you'd try to fill the hole in yourself that my vacancy would leave with hollow relationship after hollow relationship. just like you'd always done. and i would retreat into radical isolation. emotional celibacy. years spent trying to understand what the fuck had happened. your fear that i would replace you in my bed the most laughably unfounded terror imaginable.

and maybe i've done it all just to prove a point. but jesus, fuck you.

i love you so much.

and fuck. you.

10 september 2019 – march 2020

the world

the man i have a love affair with after you is as many years younger than me as you were older. this fact would have made you want to melt your skin off of your own bones. he fucks me in ways you never would have allowed yourself to; he holds my heart with grace you never had. his youth brings with it an artistry and passion that you yearned for in yourself but were too terrified of to explore.

in so many ways, my time with him felt safer than any of the moments you'd tried to keep me safe while keeping one hand on the escape hatch.

he and i meet each other in the honesty i tried to share with you, but the difference is he celebrates that truth rather than turning it to a weapon to be wielded against me. he meets my wild and allows it to unlock places in himself he long danced near but never fell into. the rawness of our reality creates a tapestry of alchemy wherein we begin to heal the damage done to us by the shame of those who'd claimed to love us before.

it will take years for the wounds left by you to heal. but there, in those hotel rooms and houseboats and apartments around the planet, doing things with him that you would have lost sleep over for years, the sprouts of my eternal future begin to see the sun.

2010

2011

2012

2013

2014

2015

2016

2017

2018

2019

2020

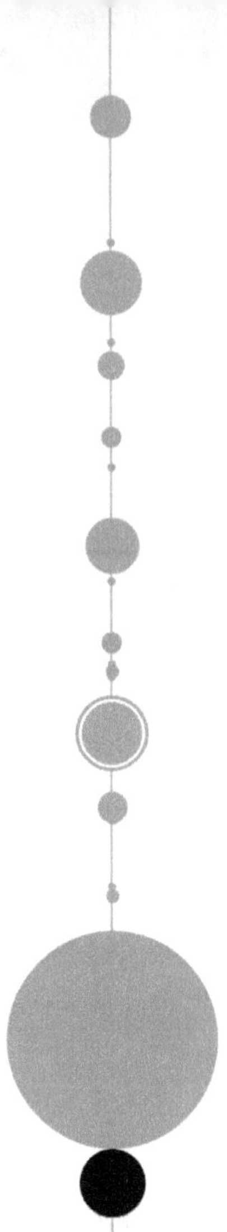

18

10 september 2019 – march 2020

dallas

austin

paris

chicago

champaign

london

amsterdam

fayetteville

guatemala

for #18, who taught me to see color again

10 september – 9 october 2019
dallas-fort worth

it was impossible to feel what i felt for you and yet the second you entered my field there i was, feeling it.

we held it at bay for a month, stealing away from the sheridan we lived in late at night to explore deep ellum and break onto hotel rooftops in downtown fort worth and sneak into the unfinished skeletons of houses in suburban development construction sites and graffiti dallas laneways with the message you had for the world. all the while, falling in passion with one another and further electrifying the physical space kept between us.

we spoke a language no one else knew and laughed together in a way i had forgotten it was possible to laugh. it was play and it was real and you met me in all of the places i needed to be met and, although i had known from the instant i saw you where it would lead, you waited for me to be ready.

as our days living in that hotel dwindled, the distance between our bodies closed.

the sneaking out we had once done to swing in the park and swim in grapevine lake became you knocking on my door at two in the morning when my roommate was sleeping at home.

the fervor we had for one another was unlike anything this life had shown me prior. the love we crafted was alchemical in a way i did not know possible.

the adventure of our open hearts and the unbound world we were launching ourselves into was poised to be one that would irrevocably ignite the fire that for so long had slumbered in my soul.

15 – 16 october 2019

5ème, paris

he puts his hand over my mouth and whispers *shhh* in my ear while he makes me come uncontrollably. our friend in bed next to us, all three of us playing the game we were set to play for the next two months. the one where we'd all pretend she slept through this every night as we traipsed around the world together sharing hotel rooms and beds and laughter so visceral the mere memory of it can make me burst out spontaneously to this day.

october 2019
suburbs, dallas

i laid across his twin sized mattress, naked atop the disheveled sheets and old, worn blankets that had undoubtedly been passed from some aunt to a cousin to his mother back to his grandma and eventually made their way to him. it seemed everything in his life had once belonged to some other family member or had been found on the side of the road and repurposed, never new and never entirely clean. i considered fleetingly how i fit into that pattern. around me, the room was hot and the air hung heavily and i wondered if its palpability came more from the perpetual texan heat outside or from the hour we had just spent with our bodies intertwined, savagely soaking in what we could of one another before time inevitably ripped us apart again.

he stood with his back to me, body completely bare except for the paint that had splattered his thighs and hands as he laid broad, formative brush strokes across the canvas that spanned the length of the wall. my heart floated contentedly in the moment we had created for ourselves and then lurched at the notion of how temporary all of this was. foolish, almost, to indulge in the fantasy knowing how soon it would all vanish. but laying there amid the creative electricity that radiated from his skin as he painted with the zeal and inspiration that our unified bodies had infused him with, surrounded by the cans of discarded colors he had found in alleyways and the clothes strewn about the floor, i felt as home as i had ever felt. a feeling i hadn't known i was missing until i had found it here, in this depressing dallas suburb with this artist who had no concept for the depth of his own skill and ability to move people.

i felt at home in a moment that was entirely, unabashedly evanescent.

we ride a train through texas
and i play you dashboard confessional
and you've never heard of them before.
in that moment i do not know what's stranger,
the fact that dallas has a functional rapid transit system
or that you are so young
you've never heard *screaming infidelities*
before.

he brings me pinecones

and i never question why.

i just arrange them on my shelf

next to pebbles i've picked up along the way

visual reminders of where i've been

who i've been

visual reminders of him.

of the notion that he sees pinecones

and thinks of me.

collects them from the earth

carries them hundreds of miles

to lay at my feet

like the selfless offering a baby makes

holding out whatever fits in their tiny hand

to the person cradling them in their arms.

> *i have brought this for you.*
> *i am not quite sure what it is.*
> *but i found it.*
> *and i find it beautiful.*
> *and all that i find beautiful*
> *i want to share*
> *with you.*

seeing the world through your eyes changed me.

i had tried to maintain a diligent watch over keeping the passion i'd always had for living alive. but two years of a shattered heart and pacing cancer wards had brought me farther away from myself than i'd ever known possible. your fervor for being helped reignite the things in me that heartbreak and living a life that wasn't mine had leadened. holding magic in my hands once more, remembering the lost importance, i vowed never to forget these things, these feelings, these passions of my heart ever again.

we flew to amsterdam and stayed in a houseboat we couldn't afford because novelty and seclusion were more important than the money neither of us had. we hadn't come to get high, we hadn't come to wander the red light district. we hadn't come here for any reason other than simply the fact that we could.

that first night we filled the whirlpool tub to the brim and i sat in the water waiting for you, my stomach sore from laughing over our dinner of baguette and hummus, my heart racing in anticipation of your body entering the same confined space as mine. as you tinkered with my camera in the other room, i considered the absurdity of sitting in a tub inside of a boat floating atop a canal, a watery russian doll allegory that charmed me as much as you did.

when you finally walked into the bathroom, you paused on seeing me. and for a moment i lurched in fear that something had changed, the way it so often does when human hearts are involved. that somehow some magic had been lost and that you would walk away from this moment, leaving me here, naked, wet, alone.

that flash of feeling scared me more than i'd have thought it would.

for that eternal second you gazed at me silently. but finally your voice drifted from you, softly asking if you could take a picture of me. if you could preserve this moment some way.

in a different life, i may have paused at the notion of my naked body being captured in a photograph. that night i didn't spare a moment to consider it. instead, my heart gave the signal to my head to nod lightly and i smiled a smile of relief, of joy, of pure contentment as you raised my phone and immortalized that feeling.

that photograph remains a favorite of myself. raw, happy, natural. i return to it when i need a reminder of the beautiful parts of life. of the things that i hold dearest to my heart. of the things that can so often drift from us if we aren't paying attention.

26 january 2020

guatemala

we talk about god in the back seat of a white van as we wind our way to the top of a volcano. you say you've stopped believing in the god they told you about. but you know something is real. you've experienced it firsthand. i watch you watching the mountains roll by out the window. taking it all in. letting it all out. losing your faith and finding it simultaneously, in that way you only can once in your life.

silence falls between us, and a voice from the front of the van suddenly says that kobe was just killed in an accident. the words hang in the air. it's one of those moments that binds strangers together, but none of us know what to do with the empty, unearned unity that's been bestowed.

three nights later you barricade us in the house. naked. stacking furniture in front of the doors. you say i must think you're crazy and i say no. i've locked myself in more rooms than you would ever believe. rigged contraptions out of whatever i could find to keep invisible boogeymen out of my bed. sometimes you just need to create a barrier between you and the monsters you know probably only exist in your own mind.

in the morning we stand naked together on the balcony and watch the sunrise over the lake as smoke billows from the volcanoes. you take pictures of me through the door as i dress. i wonder how many more of these weeks together we will have before life pulls us apart. that thought, the one i have been building barriers against entering my own mind.

your artistry and reverence for beauty showed me god in ways i did not have words for, then. the way we ate tortilla y aguacate with our hands. the way you smoked guatemalan cigarettes and trusted me to show you the world. the way we'd been so honest with each other, right from the start.

back when we were sneaking out at one am to break into construction sites, sitting on timbers in unfinished mcmansions, talking about life. back before our bodies had ever touched. always knowing we'd come together for just a fleeting moment on each others paths. a fleeting moment full of love and kindness and laughter and creation and adventure and growth. not knowing at the start just how desperately i had needed you, then.

how desperately i needed you, then.

on the flight home we sat in first class and drank mimosas and played cards and laughed until we couldn't breathe. and i don't remember the joke now but i know i was right and you know you were right and our indignation at each other's wrongness was funny in a way it only can be when you know someone so well you understand intimately why they're blind to their errors.

i wonder now if on some level i knew that that would be our last flight together. our last adventure to some far-off place. i could feel the energy of us shifting, knew some invisible reckoning must be looming. never could i have conceived that our distance would be forced by the end of the world, but in some poetic sense i think that's the only way it could have gone. a force outside of ourselves being the hand that came in to put an end to the magic of the affair that had only started in the knowing that it must not last forever. neither of us having to be the one to break the spell. history and circumstance forcing the container of our whirlwind to end as swiftly and unforeseeably as it had begun.

sealing you and me and us into a perfect moment in time, untainted by the change of our own hearts.

2010

2011

2012

2013

2014

2015

2016

2017

2018

2019

2020

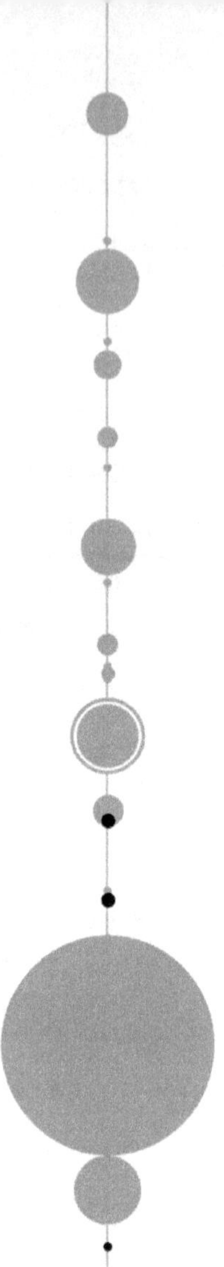

15

20 – 29 september 2016

8 – 15 june 2017

16 – 17 july 2020

    and between. and since.

queenstown, new zealand

williamsburg, brooklyn

san francisco

     for #15, who taught me there might be hope

       for american men

16 -17 july 2020
san francisco

20 february 2021
greenpoint, brooklyn

his fiancée leaves a note welcoming me to their home. it says she wishes she was here to finally meet me. it says to *have fun* while she's away. it says everything it needs to say, without actually saying it.

she's left me soap from the luxury brand she works for. it smells like rosemary and a life that isn't mine.

we haven't seen each other for three years. in that time he's lived in his car. he's fallen in love. he's gotten engaged.

in that time i've lived in four cities. i've fallen in love. i've fallen to pieces.

the world has come to a standstill and somehow here we are, still standing naked in front of one another.

our bodies remember each other across space and time. across experience. across all that's changed. so much that's changed. yet we remain a space for one another. entirely the same.

physical anchors bridging lives and worlds and timelines and realities. we eat indian food with our hands and laugh about who we used to be. who we still are. real laughs. and i realize how long it's been since a laugh came from that deep within me. it feels foreign and familiar all at once. this entire moment feels foreign and familiar all at once.

he tells me in his southern lilt that he can't wait until i meet his fiancée someday, and i say neither can i.

we revel in the beauty he's found.

there's a box of kittens under the bed. real kittens. life that has continued on in the madness of this summer where life couldn't possibly continue on.

i've never felt drawn to cats and yet they're so perfect in their newness that, just for a second, i dream of taking one home.

but i don't.

i bring nothing home.
i bring so much home.

half a year later they invite me to their wedding.
the kittens have moved on, but the world hasn't.
but the world has.
i don't go, and i'm not entirely sure why.
and i'm entirely sure why.
on their wedding day i find myself on the opposite coast, eating bagels and starting to see the future.
starting to see a life that is entirely mine.

2010

2011

2012

2013

2014

2015

2016

2017

2018

2019

2020

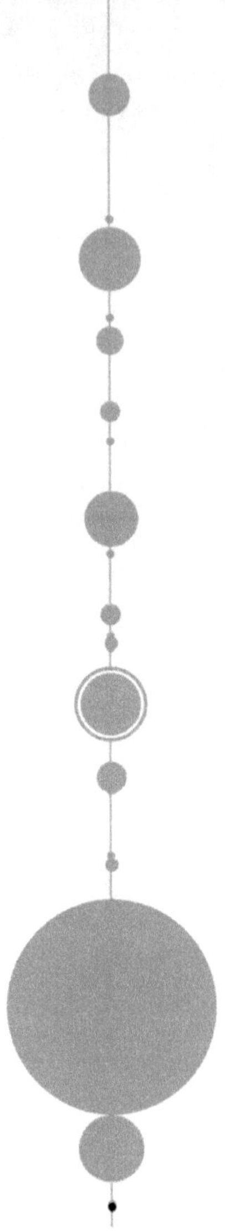

19

17 – 20 july 2020

san francisco

for #19, who taught me to let go

18 july 2020

28 august 2020

san francisco

we drive to berkley so you can buy molly from my friend's friend and of all the things i was expecting from this weekend, sitting in the same space as both of you at the same time was not it.

unwitting cuckold; california standard.

everyone's sleeping with everyone and only half the people know it.

that july afternoon, no wives or fiancées in sight.

only me. and you, and him, and his friend with the molly and the power tools and the patio we sipped beers on all afternoon and the dog who really was so sweet.

when it's time to go, he squeezes me extra tight and drawls a *have fun* in my ear as he sends me off with you. we head back south across the bay bridge, drugs in your pocket, doordash open in my palm. i reach across the car and touch the back of your neck as you drive and i'll always wonder if that was the moment that was too much.

a month later i'm back in the bay and you're nowhere to be found and i end up at a dinner party with him and his friend with the molly and both of their partners are around this time and both of their partners invite me into their beds that night. but i sleep on the sofa, just like you did. after we ate shitty mediterranean food and had bad sex and you said it wasn't me, you just couldn't sleep next to someone. so you let me sleep in your bed while you slept on the couch and i felt really fucking weird about it but everything about that summer felt really fucking weird so maybe this was just what people do. maybe some people sleep on the couch after having sex and maybe some people sleep on the couch instead of having sex and maybe some people spend their weekends fucking each others fiancés and maybe i can only fuck her fiancé when she isn't around and here i am in the middle of all of it so maybe i am some people too.

maybe i'm not cut out for california or maybe i'd been living in my head too long or maybe nothing could have felt normal that year even if it had been. and even though you faded with time, the doors you helped open stayed flung wide for years. and even though it had nothing to do with you or him or his fiancée or the friend with the molly or his wife, the crossroads had finally come. and even though you slept on the couch and were kind of an asshole, i'm so grateful to you.

he still loves me in a way that is truly so rare. and his wife still texts me asking me to come play. and that, i think, is the difference. because, yes, both of us slept on the couch.

but they still welcomed me in.

you proposed to your now-wife in the exact spot we stood, peak pandemic, and you asked me what my *thing* was and i couldn't tell you because it never mattered.

it must be traveling, you'd said.

and i said it was, and it wasn't.

the second any *thing* had started to become a badge of identifiable honor was the moment it always turned to ash in my mouth.

yours, you said, was this specific kind of electronic music. this one dj, in particular. how you went to all his shows and did molly and it really was something, this *thing* of yours.

you spoke with passion and for that i admired you but it still felt hollow, the way you were placing these fleeting moments of drug-fueled dancefloor revelations on some pedestal that defined you, while three hundred days a year you sold your soul to a company that profited off of cancer treatment.

the next day was a sunday and you had to work because you worked every sunday because they dangled a carrot of equity in front of you that kept you grinding six days a week for the money and the illusory comfort of wealth and the chance to steal away and get high on a dancefloor a few times a year that you just couldn't let go of. i left your studio apartment that the company was paying for and wandered the city on my own. found a copy of *the old man and the sea* by hemingway in a cardboard box on the street. went to a park and sat on a rock and read the whole thing.

when i got back to that studio you were still at your desk and i sat on the floor and looked up at you and told you about my day and about my book and about the things i had found.

you said you wished you could live like me.

and i knew you meant it.

and i so desperately wished for you that you would allow yourself to,
but the depth of leadened yearning in your eye told me you never would.

262

19 july 2020
san francisco

6 november 2025
london

we go to a *joe and the juice* before i even knew what *joe and the juice* was and i offer to pay as a *thank you* even though you make more in one month than i make in a year. it costs fifty dollars in a time when everything was cheap and i don't even remember what we got but i know i could carry it all with two hands.

it's been five years since that weekend that was really fun and really weird and that sent me spiraling into a tailspin that lasted god-knows how long. five years, and now i wander london and see those pink storefronts everywhere and i don't necessarily think of you every time, but the thing is i do.

i haven't been inside of one since that sunday morning in california and still, it means something.

means overpriced pseudo-health and california takeovers and how you were so kind and so human and so afraid and so cold. means the commodification of nourishment and the mass-produced illusion of novelty and how you kept your heart so wrapped in plastic that the shellshock kept me from even thinking about attempting to touch anyone else for almost four years, for how much damage your pink-hued sterility imparted on me.

but now i pass those storefronts and i don't think of you and i do think of you and it doesn't even occur to me that i could enter one. years since my body has recognized homogeneity as fuel, so long since my eyes have looked at what once was alive but had been distilled and blended and powdered and whipped and refined into something the mainstream found palpable and thought *oh, yes. that is appetizing. sign me up.*

    the millennial grey of nutrition.

    disenfranchising franchises.

    your heart that once yearned for something more.

    your cage of treacherous comfort that prevented you from tasting it.

2010
2011
2012
2013
2014
2015
2016
2017
2018
2019
2020
2021
2022
2023

17

october 2017 – october 2018

march 2019 – august 2019

and for lifetimes after that

chicago

earth

for #17, who taught me everything

28 march – 14 may 2021

costa rica

a year and a half after we'd sealed our sarcophagus i really had deluded myself into thinking your ghost had left me. that i was free.

but then suddenly there i was, peak pandemic, secretly making my way through costa rica on what was meant to be the first trip free of you or him or anyone else in years. secretly finding my feet below me once more, as the rest of the world remained shuttered inside in fear and in love and in loss.

realizing, as the path unfurled before me, that you were everywhere.

realizing, as i followed the breadcrumbs left to me by god and the sea and the man who appeared from the jungle to point me on my way, that i had come here to find you.

realizing how absolutely livid it made me, that exactly thirty-six months had passed since i'd been in colombia and all i could think about was how much i loved you and how terrified i was of my dad dying and since you'd been here and all you could think about was how much you loved me and how terrified you were of my love for you dying, and you were still everywhere. that you were waiting for me here, in the freedom i had promised myself i was finally finding.

how furious it made me, that once again, you were waiting for me in the freedom i was supposed to be finding.

the force that had connected us since time itself began had brought me, somehow, unknowingly, to the very place you had slept while you'd been in this country three years prior. my body finding herself there and my mind doing backflips wondering if i was absolutely insane to be where i was and my heart knowing the path had been laid for me by the hand that speaks only the language of the soul.

and so i spent my thirtieth birthday exactly where you had spent my twenty-seventh and i hiked the trails you had told me about and i allowed the wound that still festered deep within me from the love we had lost to reopen and start to weep her songs.

four nights later i found myself deep in the jungle once more. sitting ceremony with sacred medicine and coming to understand so much truth and so much beauty and so much love. those nights with ayahuasca held more than words will ever be able to express, but beyond the universes they opened me to, there was you. you and our story and the way we had been before we threw it all away and this deep, truest understanding of just how much you had loved me.

when the dawns came and i found myself back in my body on the floor of that temple, the love and the clarity was such that it brought unending peace and upending insanity.

seeing, so clearly, how real it had all been.

wondering, so viscerally, if this time

i had been the mad one

for throwing it all

away.

23 april 2021
diamante valley, costa rica

this is what he let me go for.

these words come to me as the sun is rising on my second night with ayahuasca. i look around and see the most beautiful bodies laying nearby me. complete strangers who i love more dearly than i've ever loved anyone. vessels for the souls they contain. in the last eight hours on the conventional clock, i have died and come back to life a dozen times. i have seen more than i have in decades prior. i have revisited myself, come home to myself. i have understood more about humanity and love and compassion than a lifetime of introspection had previously taught. i can see my future in that i can't see it at all. all i know is that i am exactly where i am supposed to be. all that i know is that he couldn't know this is where i'd find myself, but he knew i needed to find myself somewhere. and that act of love and release was the greatest thing he could have given me.

this is what he let me go for.

i manage to write these words in my journal before another wave of understanding takes over my mind, and i am again whisked away into the cosmos.

that summer back in chicago i was a crazy person and i was more sane than anyone i had ever been or known.

the layers of understanding i'd come to in costa rica had left questions that spun endlessly within me and i could spend lifetimes writing about it all and i will spend lifetimes writing about it all but for this moment all we need say is i got so lost between the cosmos and my own memory that half of me was certain you were my soulmate and half of me was certain you never existed and all of me knew i would never put it to rest until i saw you again.

in the madness and the certainty i got ready to go to a show with the friend who had been holding more than he could carry for me for years. the friend who'd befriended you, who'd lost you just as much as i had when you'd had to take an ax to all the ties to me that remained. the voice in me that had always spoken, the one i was finally too cracked open to ignore, the voice that had led me to the place you had spent my birthday, the one that had guided me along every trail i'd ever walked—that voice told me you would be there that night. and part of me was terrified and more of me just needed to put it all in the grave, whatever it even was.

and there you were, as i knew you would be, on the patio with a woman who wasn't me. and our eyes locked across the sea of bodies and i saw your fascia tighten the moment your gaze met mine. we spent the hour before the show pretending our stomachs weren't trying to come out our spines and we spent the hour of the show pretending our hearts weren't trying to escape through our chests and i had my hand clutched on a crystal in my pocket the entire time as i thought to myself *thank you for allowing me to see.*

it would have been enough, just to lay eyes on you and know that it felt but that it didn't *feel*. that you were real, but your presence didn't make me sprint to your arms. but after the show ended and we all poured back into the bar, i found myself leaving the bathroom and wading through the mass of bodies and, somehow, in a crowd of hundreds, our trajectories crossed perfectly as you were making your way to the exit with the woman who wasn't me.

and there we stood. two human beings in front of one another. two years since we'd spent a second summer falling apart.

we said our *hi*s and *it's good to see you*s and i could feel your breath not making its way past your trachea the whole time. when the most intimate of formal pleasantries had been wished upon one another, you left. the woman who wasn't me in tow. and as i watched the back of your head and the cowlick i had once loved so earnestly walk out the door, a knowing peace washed over me.

a peace that said yes, you were real. yes, we'd existed.

and yes, it was time to finally start letting you go.

26 july 2021

logan square, chicago

i sat in the grass in the middle of logan square with the friend who had been holding more than he could carry for me for years. we had just looked at an apartment together, had been talking about getting a place of our own.

the knowing voice within me had screamed my entire life that i detested this place, that i needed to flee. that i would never be free while i paced these grid-patterned concrete cages.

the brain that i had allowed to drive since the moment i chose to come back to you two and a half years before told me maybe staying here wouldn't feel like living in a waking death, if i just found a new place to live.

i had been having panic attacks at work again and my heart knew what i must do, and still the fear of listening to her and the thoughts of somehow forgetting it all and doing what i was *supposed to* were so strong they had me looking at apartments and lying *maybe this is what it's supposed to feel like*s to myself.

sitting in that grass, standing between two lives, i said to him *what if we just burned it all to the ground instead* and he said *how do you mean* even though we both knew

he knew

    exactly

what i meant.

even though we both knew

    that was

    exactly

what i was always

    meant to do.

2021

chicago

when i had said *love* before i knew you, i had meant every word.

i'd loved men, and women, and people, and places, and moments, and things and i'd loved them all as deeply as any human has ever loved.

but then i met you.

they do not have a word in english for the love i loved you with.

the love i loved you with made all of the other loves look like the stars that shine in the city. beautiful, perfect on their own.

but nothing

    compared to taking in the raw expanse

    of the unencumbered night sky,

        unadulterated

        by the constructs of man.

3 october 2021

greenville, south carolina

it's your birthday today.

i want nothing more than for you to feel loved.

and even if you don't know that that love is coming from me,

i hope you feel it.

i hope you're listening to the voices and the nudges

that began to pull at you

when you let me love you.

i hope you know

i love you

still.

after all this time.

and that while we could no longer grow together,

i hope you grow endlessly on your own.

and that, if life allows,

our vines find each other again someday.

i hope you know that loving you showed me god.

i just had no idea

what to call her

at the time.

2021

chicago

i'll always wonder which instagram post it was
    that made you block my social media.
which nightmare,
or sighting of me on the street,
or thinking about me at three in the morning,
drunk—drunk, because you couldn't do it sober,
drunk, crying on the floor,
drunk, finally swearing you'll be rid of me
    if you just sever
        that last
        tie

31 december 2021 – 15 march 2022

puerto viejo, costa rica

i moved to costa rica that winter. had left my entire life behind in november and spent five weeks in guatemala as the year wound down, but realized soon after i got there that it was wrong. that i couldn't be there, because i hadn't yet come back here. guatemala, the place i had known freedom with the man who had come after you. the one who accepted the hand i had held out to him to explore every corner of this planet of ours alongside me.

i went to guatemala because i so desperately wanted to dive back into the freedom he and i had known; to live once more in the art and the ease.

in an outdoor cave next to a volcanic lake, i sat two more ceremonies with sacred medicine, begging the gods to give me a new task, a new assignment. to rid me of the weights i knew were mine alone to shed.

but i had not yet freed myself from you.

i had not yet freed myself from any of the ghosts that clouded my soul.

and no new tasks would be bestowed until the first were complete.

and so, the plans fell apart, as plans often do when the universe has our destiny in mind. the months in guatemala i'd planned with the friend who'd held more than he could carry for me for years crumbled one morning in an instant, and the choice appeared: force a path to stay where we were, or accept the pivot that had been presented?

and so, we parted ways.

he went onward to colombia, and i went back to costa rica.

i arrived on new year's eve in the tiny coastal town that had changed everything just eight months before. i spent that first night—the last night of the year—in a hostel room, anxious over a pile of wood shavings i was convinced were bedbugs.

278

how you start a year is how you spend it, and 2022 started with a five am wake up. alone on a swing on the beach, greeting the sun while the rest of the world slept. i moved into a tiny casita in the jungle that afternoon and spent hours cleaning the mess that had been left by the previous tenants.

that night i slept in my new home under a mosquito net, entirely alone apart from the millions of wild jungle lives that buzzed and howled and sang around me.

the next two and a half months were spent almost entirely in solitude.

just me, and the howler monkeys, and the ants that found their way into every single thing in the kitchen, and my frustration with their presence, even though i was the one living in their world.

i spent ten weeks eating nothing but coconuts and lentils and a few select vegetables and doing hatha yoga and breathwork and going to meditations guided by beings who i knew understood something no one else did. i began diving, finally, into the layers of my own consciousness that i had been terrified to truly look at for years. even while i had spent those same years trying desperately to see them all.

in that tiny house in the jungle, in the country you had wandered while we had been together, in the town i had been in less than a year before, where the man had appeared from the trees to tell me where i must go—who pointed me, unknowingly, to where you had spent my twenty-seventh birthday; who pointed me, knowingly, to those first nights with ayahuasca— i began to finally do the work required to release all that i had carried since the day i was born. i began cleaning the mess that had been left for three decades. i began to release the infinite pieces of you that still wove intricately with my being. to release every binding that i had allowed, for lifetimes,

to keep me caged.

2 february 2022
puerto viejo, costa rica

i think of all of the times i have silenced the knowing voice within me, and my mind drifts back to those last months with you. when my heart was aching and i knew something was wrong and yet i didn't say anything because i didn't want it to be true. i wanted to bury it. i just wanted it to go away.

and so it grew. and grew. until it grew so big that you could see it and feel it and name it.

and if i had listened to that voice, allowed it to speak, maybe things would have been different. at the very least maybe things would have been more gentle. more humane. instead of pulling you along. making you suffer. but the logic and ration and fear in me kept me silent.

as they had done so many times before.

i had always told myself i was acting out of love, but it was fear that had truly been at the helm.

terror of feeling all i felt.

terror of feeling of all we would feel, in the wake of my admission.

terror of reckoning with the life that would come, if i spoke truth aloud.

when i ignore that voice, it feels like i'm suffocating while convincing myself i'm breathing. going through the motions of inhaling but there's plastic wrap over my face. everything is clouded, warped. i can't see clearly. just shapes and colors. and i tell myself that's the way the world is supposed to look.

even while my heart is screaming

that she cannot

breathe.

6 april – 17 april 2022
san bartolo, mexico

a year after i had inadvertently found myself turning thirty in the same place you had been as i turned twenty-seven, i spent my thirty-first birthday traveling from mexico city to a monastery in the sierra madre mountains and entering noble silence at the start of another ten-day vipassana meditation. because apparently how i intended to spend that thirty-first year was as a silent, reclusive, chaste, semi-omnipotent monk.

it had been over three years since that first meditation in sri lanka, where you had appeared, so vividly, on that sixth night. since i had been absolutely certain you had died and absolutely alone in my grieving you.

and in ways it would take me years to understand, on that night you had, in fact, died. and on that night i had, in fact, started to grieve you.

and here i was, three years later, venturing into yet another mediation with trepidatious conviction. going ever-deeper into my own consciousness, ever-deeper into the layers of my own being. trying, desperately, to extract every demon that still lurked beneath the surface.

the last time i walked these streets
    i was in a daze too.
so disconnected, yet so in tune.
then, simply survival mode.
then, at the start of so much
    that would irrevocably change
        everything.
now, entirely lost from myself.
through the haze, writing these words
    somehow brings solace.
that even in the numbness, i can find something.
that even in the numbness, i can reach through time and space
    and recognize that i am still here.
that i never left this place.
that i am here now, taking care of my current self.
that i am here now, reaching back and letting 2017 me know
    she'll survive it.
somehow, she'll survive it.
all that is. all that will follow.
and maybe i'm here in the future, too.
    feeling myself today.
knowing i loved every iteration of myself on this day
as i will know on that day.
as i might have known on that day in the past.
when everything felt
    as if it was crashing down.

vagabond summer

vagabond life

a hollow tiredness creeping below the surface

pieces that used to fit

a nap in a park

a purposeful aimlessness

an aimless purposefulness

reshaping

reimagining

revisiting, to let go

sometimes you need to go back to truly leave again

to realize that home is where the heart is.

and my heart was no longer at home.

20 june 2022
high st, edinburgh

i saw you on the street last night in edinburgh.

you were walking toward me, smiling.

i saw you on your friends instagram story last night

    in chicago.

you were at the premiere of a friends show

    smiling.

i think your new haircut is awful.

but i get it.

i had to change mine, too.

it's been three years

and i still see you on the streets of cities

    i know you've never been to.

it's been three years

and as my hair grows out,

so do the reminders of you.

but still.

i saw you on the street last night in edinburgh.

even though you were in chicago

    at a premiere

    of a show

    of a friend of yours

        i do not know.

26 july 2022
villa borghese, rome

sometimes the love i have for being alive

is the exact same love i felt when you looked at me

seeping into my cells

effervescent light that radiates out as much as it infuses back in

all at once gratitude and joy and laughter

and somehow the most beautiful, happy sorrow

december 2018
fitzroy, melbourne

january 2023
kerala, india

georgia tells me she's realized her emotions live in her hips. she's been doing pigeon pose and crying, crying. releasing.

i don't understand it at the time, yet i believe her.

i believe her, because you live in my hips. because you are caught in this liminal space inside of me, central to all i will ever create.

i believe her, because every single year since i was a child when the clock strikes twelve on new year's eve i resolve to, this year, be able to do the splits. this lifelong desire to open and stretch myself wider and wider and farther and release all that i carry and yet i have never once done the splits and to be honest i had never once even tried. decades spent saying *this is the year* and decades spent calcified.

because what would happen if all that i carry is released to the wild? what would happen, allowing myself to bend, to bend just shy of the break? to open, to open, to allow.

what would happen is that i am released back to the wild.

what would happen is that i bend, bend but not break.

what would happen is that i open, i open.

i allow.

four years later i am doubled over one bent leg, the other stretched far behind me—half-bird, half-split—and i sob as you come flooding out of me.

four years later and i still remember georgia. still remember how she told me things i did not understand, yet believed.

so many things i have not understood, and yet still i believed.

four years later, and for the first time in my life i allow my hips to stretch. to breathe.

a lifetime later, and my resolutions are finally free.

2010

2011

2012

2013

2014

2015

2016

2017

2018

2019

2020

2021

2022

2023

20

28 february 2023

goa, india

> *for #20, who taught me i didn't want*
> *to become a nun after all*

28 february 2023
arambol, goa

19 march – 2 april 2023
agonda, goa

i had never met someone who had every reason on paper to be the most interesting person in the world and yet was so truly, mindnumbingly boring.

canadian by birth but he'd spent most of the last decade living in berlin and djing at those clubs everyone talks about in berlin.

he told me about a girl he'd recently spent days on end with, who was fresh out of her first ayahuasca ceremonies and really channeling some shit. she stayed with him for a while and then things got a little crazy.

she had tried to pull him deeper but he didn't know how to get there, he'd said.

he was in india now, figuring some things out.

it was just so fascinating to me, how the actions and the world and the stories were all enough to merit a badge of beguiling cosmonaut and yet he truly seemed to just sit on the surface of it all, considering taking a step to trying to understand how to begin taking a sliver of it in.

our paths had crossed after my first-ever ecstatic dance and the silent girl who'd brought me had reconnected with a soon-to-be lover and they had stood just holding each other next to the fire for so long that this dj and i started talking. his friend, the one in the arms of mine. my friend, the one in the arms of his.

when our friends finally pulled away from each other, they made it clear their evening would end together and in so doing made it clear that our evening would end together and in that communal clarity this canadian dj offered to drive me home.

we stopped at a beach cafe so he could eat and i could watch and it was there that he told me the stories that should have made him interesting. it was in the watching and in the listening that a voice inside me spoke, *it's been nearly three years. you don't even know this piece of you anymore. maybe the stakes are so low here that it's worth venturing into. just to see.*

after his food had been eaten and his stories had been told and it was clear the night was shifting, i looked at him and said *so are you coming back to mine, then?* and we hopped on his royal enfield and back to mine we went.

he fucked like he spoke but it was enough, after nine hundred and fifty-five days, to show me that someday i would become human again after all.

but not yet.

after three years spent on a deep dive into my own consciousness and healing and spiritual planes beyond any realm of reality i'd ever known; after nearly three years of committing myself so wholly to my own journey that i thought maybe there would never be a day when another entered it; that yes, that most human desire in me still remained.

i wish i could say that it had been enough, the knowledge that that primal piece of me yet flickered in my belly. that i could have left our encounter at that and simply carried on with my story.

but the fragments of me that had not yet healed from the damage of the men who could not love me fully still roared to life after being awakened for the first time in so long.

and the truth is, even though he was the most boring person i'd ever met and i never needed to see him again, i *wanted him* to *want me.* wanted him to see in me the power and the magic that i knew from one conversation he was incapable of seeing anywhere.

but, yes, some wounded little piece of me still yearned to be desired.

even after the years of self-work.

even by someone no part of me wanted in turn.

happenstance ended us up in the same sleepy little fishing village a few weeks later. the silent girl and i were supposed to go together, but she changed her mind at the last minute to stay closer to where the now-her-lover, friend-of-the-dj was staying.

so i ended up in the sleepy little fishing village alone. and as i wandered the streets, sometimes i would pass the dj. and sometimes we would have a small little catch up. he would ask me how my startup was going and i would ask him how his workouts were going and i would observe the places within me that craved being craved and nothing beyond those brief moments on the street ever transpired again until the last night i was there.

the night before i left india he and i went to dinner, and all i remember from it is that he kept saying he needed to figure out how to use ai to make money and it was just the most dull shit a person could possibly hope to think about, let alone dedicate a life to. and something in the preposterous mundanity of it all finally freed something in me. as i walked back to my room alone, i felt the cords that had never had anything to do with him break. felt the cosmic joke laugh alongside me as the absurdity of it all finally settled itself into my cells.

the mirror he had held, so clear.

the healing i had left to do, so evident.

the devotion i had yet to excavate, so obvious.

the road to truly becoming human again, so winding.

the rawness of my liminal limerence proving herself to be the most human piece of me i simply had yet to see.

2010

2011

2012

2013

2014

2015

2016

2017

2018

2019

2020

2021

2022

2023

21

9 – 19 march 2023
   and so far beyond

goa, india

for #21, who taught me it really is possible to hold it all

twenty-one

9 – 19 march 2023

arambol, goa

you walked through the door five minutes late and the whole room had to stop to watch you come in and the second you crossed the threshold i knew you were here for a reason. knew i was sitting on the floor of that temple listening to a mad woman talk about tantric expression for a reason. had no place to speculate what that reason might be, but knew my whole body had told me you mattered the instant you arrived.

and you know that. and we've talked about it. and you've held it. and i still to this day do not know if you actually understand it, even though you say you do.

i was invisible to you for four days and i knew that. knew you were just working within the densities you carried and moving through them with the women whose orbits mirrored yours. the silent girl with the bluest eyes, whom i'd brought there with me. i was right next to her that whole week, and you literally could not see me.

until that last day. when you'd passed some barrier and broken through some plane and suddenly the field expanded and there i stood.

i'll write books about all of it and i know you know that, too.

but for now, for here, all that matters is that that door opened then. days before your birthday, in india. tantra coursing through our veins. you, spending your time with the beings and the bodies who spoke to you. me, a step removed and just being in my body while i spoke to you.

i knew then as i know now that you weren't yet done with that world. knew then as i know now that you had more scenes to play out. knew then as i know now that you could hear me, but i was still far away.

knew then that the distance was destined to someday close.

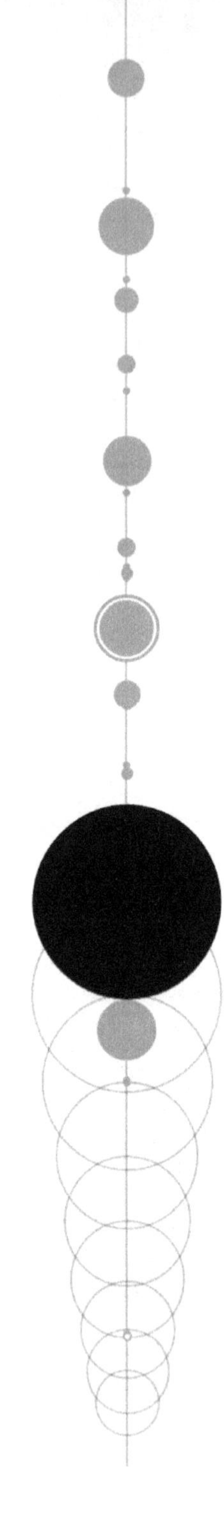

2010
2011
2012
2013
2014
2015
2016
2017
2018
2019
2020
2021
2022
2023
2024

17

october 2017 – october 2018

march 2019 – august 2019

and for lifetimes after that

chicago

earth

for #17, who taught me everything

i tried to go back to myself after you,
and i could never find her again

4 july 2023
ocean beach, san diego

i hope you're happy. oh, how i hope you're happy. i hope you found everything you couldn't find when i was clouding your sight. i hope you looked everything you were terrified of straight in the face and laughed. and cried. and realized all along you were worth all of the love the world has ever known. and realized nothing was as scary as you'd believed. and realized all you had to do was ask. i hope you took the magic we made and spun it into webs of endless spells and fairytales to dance through into eternity.

what i am trying to say is
i hope the joy we shared
was only the beginning
of the joy
you've built your entire existence around.

these days my mind is filled
     with thoughts of new york.
the nights that turned
     to sunrises.
the life lived
     before he got sick.
the life lived
          before i loved you.

20 december 2023

suburbs, chicago

i use my dad's deodorant without thinking because mine hasn't made it out of my suitcase yet. as it glides on i realize it's the same kind you always wore.

i'm home for christmas and it's been six years since we never spent christmas together and here i am, body still smelling like you. six years since you didn't want to spend a holiday together and make a memory that couldn't last and here i am, still enveloped in memories of you. five years since you called me and said *i think we made a mistake* and here i am,

still unsure

which of us

was right.

and lately,
    everyone looks like you

and i don't know what to do with that

so i eat sticky date pudding
    and wonder
    if it really was the ghost of you
    i saw
    at the evelyn last night

17 february 2024

collingwood, melbourne

if i had to go back and do it again i honestly don't know if i could survive the pain of leaving you another time. knowing now how the agony of splintering my soul into infinite broken fractals went so much farther beyond the scope of anything i could have conceived of before you. i don't know if my heart could make it through such hollow weight again without caving into dust.

but if i had to do it again, i would still do it again.

even if it meant the pain would kill me this time around. even if it meant simply allowing the pain to kill me this time. because a death from a self-inflicted stab to the chest that's grounded in truth and freedom and a love so deep it knew we both deserved better—that's a death i can sleep eternally with.

the slow death that would have come, had i stayed. the creeping, inching rot of my soul. the color draining from my world, bringing yours to the ground with me. the decay of two bodies that had long lost the life within.

that, my love, is a manner of death i simply could not bear

to live with.

march 2024

byron bay

no one gets to touch me
    unless i let them
and i had claimed that for myself
    years before you ever materialized
    into my world.

the bar was set at a height
    just shy of you
    and the fact that you could only see
    the fact that anyone had come before you
as a mark that it had been on the floor
    made me insane.

the standards for the hands that get to hold me leave billions yearning.
the price i'd put on my own flesh
    was love and respect and care and play to a degree few
    could ever attain,
    but the mere notion that any had
    made you sure my love was cheap.

at the time i tried to hold it for us both
but in the years after you
    i have had to scream it from my fascia
    to release the shame you wove in me.

this body is mine, and mine alone.

how dare you have been granted entrance

    to sacred ground

and spat on the fact

    that others

    had worshiped

    before you

2010

2011

2012

2013

2014

2015

2016

2017

2018

2019

2020

2021

2022

2023

2024

21

9 – 19 march 2023

17 – 23 march 2024

and so far beyond

goa, india

east coast, australia

earth

for #21, who taught me it really is possible to hold it all

i asked the wind for rainbows.

what she gave me

was an almighty crystalline technicolor torrent

    of cascading floodwaters

more powerful

than even my wildest

of fantasies.

6 february 2024
australia

i send you a voice note five and a half weeks before we meet up and in your reply you say you'd never heard me sound bashful before. a year of emboldened confidence, and there i was, tiptoeing towards the question i knew i'd someday ask you without ever truly seeing it.

in the year since our paths had crossed in india, our friendship had grown to hold all of the fragments we had each been before, and the wholes we were both beautifully becoming. voice notes and facetimes and a quick trip to see you in cornwall. a steady presence of proof that people like us existed, even when the worlds we found ourselves in were barren of evidence.

you had come to know every piece of me it was possible to know through conversation and observation alone, and for that i knew it would be you who came to know the pieces of me i had for so long been estranged from myself.

fate was bringing you to the same place on earth i would be and we had been planning a road trip up the coast for weeks now. as your arrival drew closer, so did my assuredness that you were the person who would bring me back from the dormancy i had dwelled in, nearly uninterrupted, for almost four years.

i floated the question to you, shyly and boldly asking you if you would be open to it. to spending that week exploring terrain entirely new for us, to holding me as i came back to life. i knew it was a lot to ask of you, and i knew you understood the gravity of all it would carry.

we discussed it for days. you, feeling receptive but wanting to make sure our friendship could survive it. me, trusting you all the more for the way you held our love on a pedestal higher than any desire for my body.

over openness and honesty and trust, we landed on *yes*. with intention and care and reverence for it all, we would spend that week diving into the physical as a means for expanding the ethereal. both the carnal and the sacred; the lust and the love.

although we had no way to know it, in so many ways i believe we both could tell that the thing we were set to open would render us entirely brand new.

28 february 2024

australia

you used the word *lovership* to describe the container. somewhere between partners and playmates and lovers and friends.

a week to commit to exploring each others depths, a dynamic created in honesty and sanctity. a space we had both danced in plenty of times before, but entered into now with the loving intention to hold and to heal and to help each other transmute.

both of us, so intimately aware of the other's shadows, of the places we could get caught.

both of us, so willing to ravage ourselves in truth,

    so ready to set ourselves

        free.

march 2024

australia

in the forty-some-odd days between that first message and your arrival, i sent you hours of voice notes. and that is not hyperbole.

every fear, every desire, every place i held shame. every single thing he had ever told me i was untouchable for. every phantom that still stirred. every thought i had had for the four years between that summer in san francisco and the australian summer i now found myself in. it was a universe of weight to unleash on you and you carried it all. told me it was okay and that you loved me and thanked me for letting you see every ghost.

i needed to lay it all at your feet and know you could hold it. needed to know if a single syllable would turn you away. needed to know that it was possible, to have every last wall down and to be wanted for what lay bare beneath the veneer.

and you proved, just as you had done for almost a year, that people like you existed.

and you proved, just as you have done ever since, that people like you are worth the wait.

10 march 2024
byron bay

i wear my mother's diamonds and a secondhand sundress i hand washed in a strangers sink as dirt ran clear from it. i text you asking you to build sandcastles with me when you arrive but the truth is i don't even need to read your response to build sandcastles.

there is a rock i have fallen in love with

in this place beyond places.

as i fall more madly into its embrace,

i grow more beautiful

by the second.

9 – 19 march 2023
arambol, goa

17 march 2024
byron bay

mars descendant, we meet
    in the throes of tantric awakening.

mars lower midheaven, we merge
    a year to the moment later.

ten thousand kilometers
    between descent
    and midheaven.

mars ruling
    mind,
    body,
    soul.

17 march 2024
byron bay

you tried to take off my dress and fumbled with the zipper and i loved the soft comedic intimacy of fumbling with someone again. the sincerity of it was one of the things i could not have told you i'd missed until i was experiencing it anew.

four years since someone had taken the care to peel back the layers that housed me.

for years unable to even consider it.

now, here.

with you.

stuck in a dress that was so long in the making of being removed.

laughing.

playing.

clothed, for just a moment longer.

the tenderness that exists

    before the taste.

17 march 2024
byron bay

you took your time and you held me and as your body hovered over mine
    you whispered,
    are you ready?
i couldn't have told you those were the exact words i'd needed you to say,
    but those were the exact words
        i'd needed you
        to say.
you said them with love and with care and with understanding,
and even through the yearning and the fear and the lifetimes of anticipation,
    i felt safe.
    knew, i was safe.
and i said *yes* and shifted my hips open wider for you
    and never took my eyes off you
    never taking your eyes off me.

17 march 2024

byron bay

the feeling of feeling,
    for the first time,
something i had felt i'd felt
    a million times
    before.

17 march 2024

byron bay

you looked at me

with the eyes you use

when i know

    you can see

18 march 2024

byron bay

at dinner i wear a red dress and you speak french and the current running through you can be felt three tables away. you take a picture of me smirking sitting across from you with the cheap disposable i'd given you for your birthday. days later, lives later, i will use that same camera to capture you, naked on the floor. tarot cards spread before you, your heart on my sleeve. body still so new to me, yet so eternally ingrained.

i had known this is how it would feel,

and yet i never could have prepared

for this.

19 march 2024
byron bay

the air is the same as the feeling.

perpetual summer.

heat that hangs in your skin.

sitting on curbs with you

eating breakfast.

bodies smelling of each other.

smelling of the chemical change

that occurs when sun meets flesh,

transforming bodies from beige to life.

smelling of the chemical change

that occurs

when flesh

meets flesh.

transforming bodies from death to life.

two to one.

you to me.

you,

to me.

19 march 2024

byronshire

we spent our days playing mermaids in waterfalls

rubbing silt on each other's faces

squishing mud between our toes

the play, we'd said, we'd always yearned for

the love, we knew, we'd never known

20 march 2024
surfers paradise

we play around with *whore* and *slag* and *filthy little slut* and honestly i hate it all and honestly when you say it with authority and grab the hair at the nape of my neck i've never loved anything more. most times it feels electric but one time it makes me break down and i'm scared to tell you we went too far and poked something that had never stopped bleeding but you hold me and hold me and hold me and say *it's okay baby i've got you.* after twenty minutes in your arms you kiss me and, whispering, ask if it feels safe for you to get up and get some of the chocolate i'd bought for you and i say *yes.* and with the care of cradling something more delicate than fragile you pull yourself from beneath me and walk to the kitchen to bring me those chocolates. you crawl back into bed and hold me once again and select one made with rose and ask if that sounds nice and *yes,* that sounds so nice.

you feed it right to me and the cacao pulses through my veins and when my breathing has finally steadied you ask if you can help wash this from me. you guide me to the shower and i couldn't have walked there without your arms to steady my gait; couldn't have moved through any of this without you to hold the weight.

you turn the water on and i'm still shaking but you keep your hands tight around me while you kneel on the marble and take a cloth to my skin and wash my body with the tenderness of a parent caring for their sick child. it takes time and it takes patience and it takes love i have never known, for you to be on the floor of that shower, cleaning the invisible dirt from my soul.

you ask if you can wash my hair and again i say *yes* and as you work shampoo through my strands, i realize no one has ever done this for me before unless it was their job. three weeks shy of thirty-three, and yours are the first hands to touch me in this specific way. in a way that is more intimate than any of the moments we had shared before. you ask me questions about how to make sure you're doing it right and if you're being gentle enough and you use the voice you use for kindness. low, soft, but so strong i know it can carry whatever comes. it is a tone that says *you are safe, you are loved, you can melt. close your eyes, and know i will kill any demons who dare arise.*

when all of the bubbles have washed from my brain and down the drain, you step out and pick the biggest towel in the room. you hold it open for me as i move onto the mat and you wrap it around my whole body like i am three years old. and i am three years old.

again on your knees, you use it to dry me like i am incapable of doing it myself, and in that moment i am incapable of doing it myself.

but all i have to do is stand there.

when my body is dry you envelop me again and we go back to the bed and get under the covers and you say we can stay there as long as we need to. we'd had plans that day and i don't even know what they were but every fiber of you made it clear that *here* was the only place we needed to be.

it seems so simple to me, now. to be loved in that way. to be given the grace and the space to melt and cry and say without speaking,

> *some invisible thing inside of me that has festered*
>
> *for three decades is collapsing, and i cannot breathe.*
>
> *i know we're supposed to go outside soon but there are*
>
> *rats made of ice running underneath my skin and*
>
> *it only feels this way when it's about to feel really*
>
> *bad and i do not trust my legs to walk me anywhere.*

to lay that at someone's feet and to be cradled in the grief of simply feeling. to be kept safe by someone who had promised to keep me safe.

it seems so simple to me now, because you made it so simple then.

and it was the most profound thing i had ever experienced.

you carrying what i carried, while caring for me.

transmuting, with simply your being, my understanding of what it means to be loved.

20 march 2024
surfers paradise

we held each other's hands over the table at lunch as you told me things you had never told another soul and i told you i loved you, shadows and all.

in the density of our emptied plates, i said *what if...* and you interjected *...we got ice cream and went back to the room?* and i said *how did you know?* and you said *our inner children are very similar* and my heart did a backflip and for ice cream we went.

we took a photo there, in front of the gelato shop where you first learned you're allowed to ask for free tastes. smiling through the weight of that day.

diamonds around my neck, you standing beside me.

only three days in, already so much coming out.

21 march 2024

sunshine coast

we played dinosaurs and the kangaroos loved you and we were beaming far wider than any of the children we passed. we were laughing in ways i'd forgotten possible, in a way you only can when your shared humor is such that no one else on earth would understand the joke. but there you are with someone, weeping for how excruciatingly hilarious it all is to just you two. in a way that is layered and clever and astute and compounds over time, calling back to itself in a game that never ends, getting funnier all the while.

as we walked you told me stories of your trips to america, how you'd found yourself in some of the less-traveled places. and as the tales unraveled we realized your path had wound you to my university town, years after i'd left. you'd spent your few days at a pub in fitchburg off fish hatchery road, just around the corner from a summer job i'd had in 2011. the summer someone nothing like you had spent telling me i was nothing and the summer i had nearly believed every word.

the magic of the tag game we'd been playing around the globe made the whole day glow all the more. that same vacation had seen you drive through buffalo, and i scoffed for how much i hated it there. you said it was one of the most surreal places you'd ever been, how you were sure the hotel you'd stayed in had been run by the mafia. and i said *yeah there's some wild places up there* and you joked about chintzy pseudo-italian decorations and waitstaff sent directly from brooklyn. i echoed back the experience—plastic grapevine hung from the ceiling, styrofoam pillars in the lobby, and mirrors on the ceiling.

as we mused on the absurdity of such places, the details became far too fine, the knowledge way too personally experienced. we looked at each other in shared quizzical wonderment as the realization dawned on us that we were describing the same seedy hotel off i-90, the one i had involuntarily spent nights of my life in during my stint as a flight attendant. the one you had somehow chosen and paid for, despite the gaudy photos and horrific google reviews.

and suddenly there, on the other side of the planet—after a friendship that had spanned three continents in a year—we realized we had slept in the same garish place just months apart, years before our threads had ever knowingly weaved.

you looked at me with the eyes you use when you are coming to understand something, something you knew i already knew.

this pull i had felt to you since that first moment in india.

the magic that went beyond coincidence.

this connection that was lifetimes deep.

22 march 2024

caloundra, sunshine coast

you made a nest on the ground of blankets and pillows, played the kind of music that was right to play. you told me this act was devotional, that it would end before we enacted the scene that, in just five day's time, i had grown so accustomed to playing out with you morning, noon, and night.

simply receiving was foreign, a discomfort in my bones at the thought of you giving with no expectation of my body in return.

that, you said, was why i needed this.

that, you said, was what you wanted to give.

we sat across from one another, bodies bare, eyes locked, and simply gazed upon each other for a lifetime.

when all the barriers had fallen, as staring into someone's soul causes them to do, you brought our bodies closer, eventually, to touch. my legs wrapped around you, hearts and foreheads together, you held me in your lap as our breath flowed out from one of us and into the other. energy moving from being to being, souls dancing and playing as one.

you held me like that—just breathing, just beating—allowing safety to internalize and walls to come down. you said the words *i've got you* and in more than one way, i knew you did.

when you could feel i had softened enough to be moved, you helped me lay down and melt into you even more. for an hour, you touched my body in a way that said *i love you*, in a way i had never before known. hands moving over flesh, weights being lifted by the gentleness of your care. an intimacy beyond devotion; a tenderness beyond compare.

you ended the morning with gratitude—for me, for our love, for this week we had shared.

and mine, in turn, for the mountains you moved, for the stories in me you rewrote. for the way you knew, even better than i, all i needed. and the way you gave it all with not a single thing asked in return.

22 march 2024

sunshine coast

you asked me what it had felt like, when you'd walked into that room in arambol the year before. when every piece of me knew instantaneously that you were here for a reason.

i told you it was a wall of certainty, this physical sensation throughout my whole body, this current within my entire soul.

one i have only experienced with a handful of people.

one that has always been right.

soul and body, speaking their languages as they so oft do. soul recognizing a counterpart she has known eternally, body experiencing your presence for the very first time. mind, the one catching up. understanding their whisperings, translating through sensation: *that person matters.*

that connection to your soul, i said, in some other realm, is one i'd continued feeling over the year. but only when you were up there. this feeling of you in the cosmos that i could not really explain. tangible, when the version of you on earth chose to be living in a manner that furthers you. vanishing, when you got bogged down in the mundane.

this week, i'd said, you had been mostly up there. this higher form of you, dancing through timelessness with me. but i could feel you dipping, could feel you wane.

yours to choose, i'd told you, if you would ever join me there.

yours to decide, if on earth you would stay.

he only expressed frustration with me that once. on the beach in queensland. me, trying desperately to articulate how hard it was to articulate. the places he took my body to. the places he made come alive within me. how good it felt, feeling him.

he only got frustrated that once.

voice elevated, imploring in exasperation and command, *i am not in your body. i do not know these things unless you tell me.*

he had had every piece of me for so long and still, my voice faltered when it attempted to bridge the realms between what felt and what was physical.

still, the deepest truths of my experience were incapable of freeing themselves from my soul.

22 march 2024

caloundra, sunshine coast

bodies still intertwined, i can't tell which heartbeat is mine

they both pulse through me

they both give me life

hand on his heart, head cradled perfectly

my eyes look up and find his

 i'm going to write poems about you, you know that right?

he kisses my forehead, that space on my face left so wonderfully open,

forever awaiting the kind of kiss that brings the love no other does,

squeezes me closer to him, as he says

 i know.

and i have never

known peace

like this.

23 march 2024

west end, brisbane

we had known the week would only last a week and yet somehow after six endless nights, our week together was ending.

as you packed your bags you asked if i would be alright once you'd gone, and i said *i think so* and i'd meant it.

although the way you'd infiltrated every cell of my being had gone so much further than i ever could have dreamed, i knew the time had come for solitude. to integrate all we had opened.

i knew it would be complicated and i knew i was tangled in you, but i knew we would continue to hold each other as we evolved into whoever we'd become in the wake of this. and beyond anything i knew the evolution was simply part of the process. that the feeling and the love and the cavern it would all leave was necessary to the transformation taking place.

i knew that stepping into forever meant letting this version of you go.

letting you go back, while i continued forward.

letting you go, in order to begin the life that awaited me on the other side.

23 march 2023
west end, brisbane

i have not felt emptiness

in someone's wake

in a very

long

time.

23 – 24 march 2023

west end, brisbane

i draw the blackout curtains and tell myself i can sleep until eleven and that'll be okay. my body needs it and i have nowhere to be.

at five thirty my limbs start instinctively feeling for you, reaching for the naked body i've grown so accustomed to awakening with mine, in the span of just six eternal nights.

24 march 2024

south bank, brisbane

fourteen hours have passed since you left.

i've showered and eaten and slept and brushed my teeth three times.

    and still, my lips smell like you.

someone walks by

    and they smell like you.

    and you smelled different every day.

      i had forgotten what this kind of hollow felt like.

      the kind of hollow that only excavation can leave.

it rains and i seek shelter in a pagoda and as the wood dampens, it smells like you too. i wonder if it's the sal or if it's just that you have crept into a layer of my soul i had not anticipated.

the one where scent twirls through memories that pull at my heart and back to my consciousness.

    an ever-connected weaving web

      of emotion

      and feeling

      and yearning

      and peace.

1 april 2024

cairns

i see a red dot pop up and find my mind hoping that it's you

find my heart sink when another name appears

and the thing is

i know it actually has nothing to do

    with you

and everything to do

    with me

and whatever need i still have

to feel wanted

    validated

    desired

    by an external force

there are so many things happening in your world

so many facets crumbling to the sea

why would i even want to be near

    the devastation

knowing

all too well

my presence would solely exist

    to help you

pick up

the pieces

20 april 2024
cherry hill, seattle

i feel myself wanting to give you love,

but my love

finding

no home

in you.

2010
2011
2012
2013
2014
2015
2016
2017
2018
2019
2020
2021
2022
2023
2024

17

october 2017 – october 2018

march 2019 – august 2019

and for lifetimes after that

earth

for #17, who taught me everything

seventeen

26 april 2024
cherry hill, seattle

the day after i meet a stranger i know will become a friend, i buy the sparkling water we used to always get from trader joe's

for the first time in years.

just to see if it still tastes like you.

and it does.

and it doesn't.

and suddenly i understand

why

i had

to come here.

2010

2011

2012

2013

2014

2015

2016

2017

2018

2019

2020

2021

2022

2023

2024

21

9 – 19 march 2023

17 – 23 march 2024
   and so far beyond

goa, india

east coast, australia
   and so far beyond

for #21, who taught me it really is possible to hold it all

3 may 2024

cherry hill, seattle

five and a half weeks after you left me in west end, we facetimed for three hours.

as we laid in bed together, half a world apart, you said that maybe we had been blind to the perfection of it all. that you had never before laughed that hard or been challenged the way i challenged you. maybe we were fools for thinking the container of a week was all we were meant to share. you said maybe we really were supposed to be together, after all.

that, maybe, *we'd made a mistake.*

and wouldn't you know how good it felt, hearing you say that?

and wouldn't you know how readily my heart jumped on it, the idea that someone i loved wanted me again.

but it was a pattern of mine, don't you see? walking back through doors my soul knew were closed.

it was a pattern of mine, i assure you, hoping the present could recreate what had passed.

it was a pattern of mine most painful, looking my future in the eye and turning away from her when the red herring of immediate attachment reappeared.

and it was a pattern of yours, i well knew, grasping onto any love given.

and it was a pattern of yours, you'd oft told me, creating wives from mere glances.

and it was a pattern of yours, i had witnessed, staying long after you ought to have gone.

but there we were, as far out from the end of it as we'd been from the start, having a conversation about *going back.*

my heart still loved you and my wounds still festered in such a way that you cracking that door cracked something in me. all while knowing, while you really did love me, this scene was a reenactment for us both. that walking through that door would replay the narratives we were both ready to rewrite.

you, filling some void with the love i gave.

me, filling some void by giving it.

4 may 2024
cherry hill, seattle

when you left

i'd thought

you were gone

5 may 2024

cherry hill, seattle

i feel myself wanting your words and your voice and your hands.

part of me knows you are not who you need to be, yet.

that we both have a lot left to do.

you have an entire reality to burn down.

and my eternal future is just starting

    to materialize.

but still.

    it is nice to be loved.

and so nice

    to be loved

    by you.

5 may 2024

cherry hill, seattle

do we love each other?

or do we love who the other shows us

   in ourselves?

6 may 2024

orcas island, san juan islands

i am shifting so rapidly.

you are invited.

but i will not wait.

i cannot wait.

8 may 2024
orcas island, san juan islands

how many times
do i have to let you go
before i get
to keep you?

8 may 2024

orcas island, san juan islands

i pace around the driveway,

talking to you a world away,

my parents sitting inside.

envisioning, all the while,

the christmas day on which

you might someday meet.

9 may 2024
orcas island, san juan islands

have our timelines intertwined?
or have they simply intersected?

2010
2011
2012
2013
2014
2015
2016
2017
2018
2019
2020
2021
2022
2023
2024

17

october 2017 – october 2018

march 2019 – august 2019

and for lifetimes after that

earth

for #17, who taught me everything

you were in my dreams last night.

    again.

you were him. and you were you.

how is it fair that you get to be him now too?

i had told you we could try it again

and the second i saw you i knew

    i'd made a mistake.

you weren't who i wanted you to be.

    or maybe you were

but i wasn't who i thought i was

    anymore.

i waited for him at the bar and asked if they had

anything without alcohol

and the bartender laughed callously and said *no*.

i was sitting across from myself and that external version of me said

that's okay, maybe it would be nice to have one.

it had been so long.

maybe it would be nice.

to try it again.

    just one drink.

for old times sake.

and the version of me i was still sitting in screamed at her.

    screamed.

i can't remember ever screaming like that

    in a dream.

and i was screaming at me.

the bartender told me to relax, it was fine.

    one wouldn't hurt.

the me outside of me seemed torn.

the me i was, was desperate.

pleading.

so sure of my sanity i felt absolutely insane.

    do not go back.

    you cannot go back.

not even one.

me and the me outside of me ordered food instead.

thought we should wait for you but didn't know how long you'd be.

i felt guilty as i ate.

for not letting myself go hungry for you, i felt guilty.

but then you arrived at three am and said you'd eaten a steak at the airport.

    could have gotten here sooner but wanted that steak,

        years of vegetarianism be damned.

wanted the french fries covered in animal fat.

forewent time with me

to eat that airport steak.

and i didn't feel guilty anymore.

you ordered whiskey neat just like you always drank at home

    but everything about you was wrong.

you were you and you were him and you were wrong.

and i couldn't believe i had almost waited for you.

couldn't believe i had almost poisoned myself for you.

i told you i had plans the next day but we could find each other later

    but really all i needed was air.

    space.

i spent the day walking alone through crowds of people who seemed so unaware,

> so lost in their own grey worlds.

feeling trapped.

feeling so outside of it all and somehow held within it.

as i walked, my legs remembered

> they could fly

as though the sheer movement of wandering

had liberated a memory locked within them.

and i allowed myself

to lift off.

in the middle of a piazza, flying off the ground.

hundreds of people around me, not a soul looking up.

> except one.

a man i have never met

whose instagram i found two years ago

when nothing made sense.

> but he made sense.

and he stood there watching me and smiled.

and i was afraid of the height but i kept going higher.

and i was afraid of descending because descending meant facing you.

when i finally came back to earth i walked to our meeting point and my heart was racing and my mind was so heavy and i was so afraid of hurting you.

> again.

but i knew i couldn't pretend anymore.

and the second you saw me you started to cry.

the same tears you cried the day you first truly realized it was over.

the day we both knew we could never come back from.

you stood there heaving and my heart shattered again.

and i told you the truth.

i told you i couldn't go back.

told you my heart had long grown on.

    and that i was so sorry.

for ever dragging you into any of this.

but this time.

    finally.

for once and for all.

    i needed to let myself fly.

10 may 2024
san juan islands

i stand on the back of the yakima and feel your ghost wrap his arms around me and finally i cry. finally i release you. finally after lifetimes lived, i leave you behind. i leave you here. i die, one last death.

and leave you

in the grave.

2010

2011

2012

2013

2014

2015

2016

2017

2018

2019

2020

2021

2022

2023

2024

21

9 – 19 march 2023

17 – 23 march 2024
and so far beyond

goa, india

east coast, australia
and so far beyond

for #21, who taught me it really is possible to hold it all

11 may 2024
cherry hill, seattle

last night i spent an hour drawing a picture of us as octopuses

not octopi

but intertwined octopuses

tentacles wrapped around each other

me, plastered to the top of your head that is also your body that is also

your stomach that is also your heart

me, touching as much of your octopus body with my octopus legs as i can

drawn inside a card i bought for you on an island i visited with my parents

an island i went to to open the space in my heart for new love to enter

i drew this drawing in a card to send it to you on the other side of the world

    so that maybe you would feel me

    more than you already do

today i stopped four separate times

to pick four different kinds of wildflowers

a daisy

a bluebell

a little red one whose name i don't know

and a purple one that grew on a vine

i pressed them between the pages of my journal

so that i could put their colorful bodies inside the octopus card

and send them to you on the other side of the earth

with love

biohazards be damned

i spent my day picking flowers for you

with my human hands

with my octopus arms

with my octopus heart that lives in my stomach that is also my head

i picked you flowers a world away

and maybe

just maybe

that means

i love you in a way

neither of us

had anticipated.

16 may 2024
5ème, paris

it's four am and i'm wide awake.
if you were here and it was your birthday
i'd be writing you a card in the other room,
    telling you how much you mean to me.

but you aren't here.
and it isn't your birthday.
so instead i write these words,
    and wonder about our fate.

how far into forever can i feel you?
am i blind to the work you've left to do?

would you come to the jungle with me?
sit on the floor around a fire and sing?

will you be the you
    i've felt you
    able to be?

may 2024
5ème, paris

things were murky but i'd known they would be.

this gnosis in my body and mind of all you could choose to become, this whispering in my soul that said you had long left the cosmic realm in which we first met.

wishing, so desperately, that you would return there. float back up to neverland and meet me, once more, in the beyond.

experiencing, so repeatedly, that you were remaining earthbound. rooted down in humanity, with no sign of giving up life.

once more, my soul knew i must soldier on.

once more, my heart screamed her song as i relearned, in anguish, to listen.

22 may 2024
siera nevada, portugal

i love you i love you i love you i love you

and why

does it make me

want

   to scream

26 may 2024

siera nevada, portugal

when i told you that all i'd ever wanted was for someone to come with me, i meant you. i meant you were invited to this life. you, who played with me so effortlessly. you, who loved me so deeply. once.

but the next night you ran into your twice ex'd of a lover.

and chose to go back.

while i blazed ahead

alone

once more.

loving you was peeling an orange with my bare hands

tearing back layers, zest flying

revealing the sweetest, sourest flesh within.

sun-ripened.

voraciously devoured.

acid burning under my fingernails long after they'd clawed

 their way through your skin,

stinging parts of me that had never before been touched.

so sensitive, so fresh, suddenly so alive with pain.

the remnants a searing reminder

of the bounty we'd feasted upon.

the burn

 worth every bite.

the night of the day the spell breaks

i instinctively set fire to sage

as i enter the bedroom.

hands moving without thought.

tiniest flame engulfing the dust green leaves

smoke billowing up, embers blazing red.

realizing only as the scent fills my senses

    that i am clearing you.

that i have gotten to such a place where,

reflexively,

i clear you.

heart bearing the weight and, still,

    release.

as i dance naked around the bed

and for the first time

in months

do not imagine you

in it.

30 may 2024

siera nevada, portugal

i call a stranger's dog *baby* and suddenly my mind is flooded with you.

baby. baby. baby. it's okay, baby.

how no one had ever called me that before. how i had never let myself be held by someone so softly that the word *baby* felt right. how being somebody's *baby* before you felt like a trap. how you cradled me in your arms that morning after you'd made me come so hard it broke me and i cried and cried and you said

don't worry, baby. you're safe. i've got you.

how i knew that you did.

how i let you have me.

how never in a million years could i have imagined that in just one week, a word that i had held at such intentioned distance

for my entire life

could be entirely

redefined.

it is art.

all of it.

don't you see?

the way she leaned the rusted wheelbarrow against the shed.

the way i could smell you on me,

hours after your plane had left the earth.

the way i put on a dress i'd bought for you

and noticed it was shorter now.

not for it having shrunk,

but for how my body

had grown.

the art of a life,

truly being lived.

the art of the mundane,

truly being loved.

spring and summer 2024

earth

the moment you reopened the doorway to the thing we'd felt in march, every piece of me seized onto it. simultaneously knowing that we were not meant to be, and also wondering, as you were, if maybe we truly were destined for one another.

as soon as it felt like it was on the table, the deepest attachments within me flooded open and told my mind that i wanted all of you. every single piece. and the reality is, you gave me more than any human being had ever given me before. you continued to hold me in ways i had never been held. you listened to my laments and my confusion and my processing with earnestness and care and a heart that saw me in ways i didn't know it was possible to be seen.

and still, i wanted more.

you held me at the exact distance it was right for you to hold me, a distance that was interwoven with almost every single piece of your heart.

the feelings and the words and the way i screamed you into the night for months to follow have absolutely nothing to do with you and they have absolutely everything to do with you.

you, the soul and the being who were finally massive enough to unlock these torrents, these revelations. you, the human who is so expansive in your love that you are able to hold it all as it comes cascading down. you, the mirror for all of the shadows i was finally ready to bring to light.

and you, simply you.

friend, lover, human, man.

6 june 2024

lake como

my heart is so in love
it feels lighter than air
and made of lead
simultaneously

8 june 2024
lake como

before sleeping last night i get a message from a former lover

telling me i look like a fire emoji

in a recent video i've posted.

his girlfriend sends me a message

asking when i will see them again.

saying they miss me.

i wonder

    if she knows.

or if that fire emoji

would burn down

their entire relationship.

i awaken to a friend in my bed

    shirtless.

as i try to get up, he pulls me in

closer than he ever has,

hands running up and down my body.

he has never done this

    before.

eleven years of friendship,

countless beds shared,

and here,

on this morning,

    he decides he wants to have me.

i allow him to feel my skin, but all i can think

is

    he is not you.

he, who is so tenderly needing my flesh.

he, who loves me so.

he, who is right here in this bed slowly pulsing himself against my still-clothed body.

all i would need to do

is tilt my hips,

part my lips,

give one sign

he can proceed,

and he would do

anything

i ask.

instead,

i sit up,

kiss his hand,

and leave him

alone in his yearnings.

his skin

does not feel

like yours.

i make myself coffee

in the little italian percolator

on the gas stove,

sit on the balcony he paid for,

look at my phone,

see five messages

from a man nine thousand miles away

asking

if he leaves his job,

can he come

and be with me?

   just for a little bit.

he would quit his job

and fly across the globe

to be with me.

   just for a little bit.

and i do not even reply.

because he

is not

   you.

you have not spoken to me in almost twenty-four hours,

and without knowing why

   i know why.

when my phone finally flashes your name,

the message says

you went on a date last night,

had fun with her

well into the hours of the morning.

so much fun

your housemates

   are livid.

four men

in ten hours.

three,

who would risk everything

for the chance to touch me,

   even for just a little bit.

you,

whose useless messages i await

like a pathetic dog in the pound.

loving family after loving family

passing me by

saying *oh she could be the one.*

and while i may be the one for them,

you,

tragically

    only you,

appear to be

    the sole soul

i want

    to take me

    home.

8 june 2024
lake como

i stroll past george clooney's house

and talk to you on the phone

about your date

about your night

about the apologetic conversation you're going to have to have

    with your housemates

it is the first time

that speaking to you

has ever felt disconnected

like we really have landed

    in two different universes

i hear my voice saying words, but i am not entirely certain

    who is speaking them

i am still so wrapped in you

    and you are still so wrapped

    in a world

    that seems

      so alienly human

10 june 2024

cinque terre

you.

who have infiltrated all of my senses.

you. the new barometer

by which all touch will be measured.

you.

through whom a current runs

connecting your soul

eternally

to my flesh.

tomorrow i may lose my mind
for all the ways in which
i do not know.

for today
it is enough
simply to know
that you love me.

the simplest
and most complex
    knowing
    and not knowing
i have ever
    known.

11 june 2024
florence

i sink my teeth into my own skin and imagine the bite is coming
from your mouth.
what would i give
to have you here?
to feel you
sunken so deeply into my body,
devouring all that i am?
teeth and bones and claws
kneading me.
teeth and bones and claws
as far beneath the surface
as they can be.
needing me.
what would i give
to you?
a pound of flesh.

a pound of flesh
for a pound
of flesh.

14 june 2024

florence

i do not know how much more
my heart can take.

i do not know
how to accept any less.

14 june 2024
frankfurt

i'm hemorrhaging you
and you have no idea
there's even a wound

14 june 2024
frankfurt

i don't know how to let you turn into a memory

but i know i have to.

because even now,
that's all you are.

you haven't lived up to my memory of you
since the memory was formed.

and still i sit
    hopeful
you'll return.

fool me once.
fool me twice.
fool me in perpetuity.

shame on no one
    but me.

15 june 2024

frankfurt

a single drop of blood on the crispness of white hotel sheets and instantly my senses are flooded with you. how we left so much blood in that hotel bed we joked that housekeeping would think we'd done some kind of ritual sacrifice. how maybe it really did feel like we'd done some kind of ritual sacrifice. how much none of it felt like sacrifice, offering everything i had to you.

body. blood.

take it all.

just give me all you have in return.

it's not that i want you to be
    more than who you are.
it's that i want you to see
    all that i know you can be.

the thing is i love you

and the thing is i know i deserve better.

    maybe not *better*.

    maybe that's not fair to you.

i know i deserve *more*.

that you love me and hold me and cherish me

    as much as you are willing to

it's just that the depths that i need

    could drill antipodes in the earth

    and still come out the other side

        yearning.

17 june 2024
germany

do you miss me?
have you even noticed
i'm gone?

and maybe i am a lot. maybe it is exhausting to be with someone who doesn't know how to feel partially. if i love you i love you with every atom of my soul. when i play i am taken over by the genuine child who lives within my bones. and when the sadness comes it consumes my waking days. bereft. leadened. complete in its maddening. i do not know what is normal. i do not know how others feel, or how they don't. all i know is that this human life of mine demands to be felt. to be experienced on every plane. that i would take guttural sobs so deep they make me fear i may never breathe easily again over the numbness of nothing. keep your pills away from me and let me reach into my own belly and pull out the rot. let me clear these wounds with my own hands and hold myself while i wail.

yes maybe it is a lot. but i do not ask you to carry it. i do not ask you to make this pain your own.

all i ask is that you grieve your grief alongside me. that you play with tenacious ferocity with me. that you love as miraculously as you possibly can, all that you love.

all i ask is that if we grant each other the gift of our love, please oh please, let that love consume the darkness and burn light into our hearts.

19 june 2024

germany

we spent two hours speaking to each other through a screen today. faces two dimensional, hearts in the beyond. i told you i was tangled in you, more deeply than i'd anticipated becoming. that i knew it had nothing to do with you, and yet the things you were bringing up in me continued to be immense. that i knew it had everything to do with you, but only the *you* i'd met in some other place. the version of you i'd felt you able to be, seen you able to be, that i so longed for you to let yourself become.

and you said *i know* and i knew you did.

and you, as always, listened as i tried to unweave the tapestry of my past wounds that had been woven decades before you had ever floated into my world. and you, as always, held every single piece i held out for you to hold.

these little damaged shards that the mirror of you allowed me to see. these fragile broken pieces that the love of you allowed me to mend.

you asked me how i was doing with you having met someone else, and i answered in all honesty that it was both bringing up a lot of discomfort, and that my heart was so endlessly happy for you.

i asked you what she knew of me and you said *she knows everything.*

you had told her our entire story, had made sure she understood the sanctity of our love. and she had found it beautiful, that you had a person such as me in your life.

you said you and i were free to keep being exactly who we are together.

you said she couldn't wait to meet me someday.

and i said the same about her.

and in my soul i felt unending love for both of you.

and in my heart i felt the remnants of past pain, asking to finally be freed.

19 june 2024

germany

i can't even shower without thinking of you.

without wanting you there,

    somewhere there with me.

in this shower that's too small for even me,

wanting you here.

wanting the gravity of you taking up space

    i don't even have.

wanting to clean myself

    through dirtying myself

    with you.

wanting to feel your skin on mine.

    wet. warm. alive.

proof that there is more

    than this vacancy

    in which i dwell.

19 june 2024
germany

and sometimes i can't help but wonder:
        does your heart
                write poems about me
        the way mine
                writes entire pages
                        about you?

21 june 2024
frankfurt

i'm mad at you. i'm mad at you. am i mad at you? or am i livid with me?

21 june 2024
frankfurt

my tummy hurts when i see your name in my messages but there isn't a reply.

and that's how it feels.

not that it makes my stomach lurch with grief and longing,

not some grandiose poetry on yearning and bellyaches.

just that my tummy hurts.

this childlike pain, disembodied from my mind.

a manifestation of all you aren't.

your absence causing the space within me

that is five years old

to want

to cry.

respect yourself enough

to stop

holding

on.

23 june 2024

tuscany

i am relearning
the vulnerability
of love

24 june 2024

tuscany

on wednesday i told you i would take more of you, if you were able to give it. but that i understand if you can't right now. you give me so much, and here i am wanting more. insatiable to the love you fill this world with. i don't know what more there is to give, and still. i would take it.

constantly, i am able to convince myself you are ready to leave me. ready to walk away from me because i have become too much for you. and i know that that would be okay. that if you were to feel that, then by god it is best that you should leave. and even knowing it would be best, my tender heart squeezes in anticipatory pain of the day you say *i just can't anymore*.

but instead what happens is that you send me a voice note. three and a half minutes long. telling me all about your weekend and the sun and how the dj was good but the sound system was bad. how you made breakfast with friends that morning. and my heart tumbles at the beauty of you, thirty-eight years old, still waking up at a friends house after a saturday night. all making breakfast together and lounging in the morning light.

am i ready for those mornings again, too?

at the end of your musing you thank me for giving you insight into my thoughts. into my feelings. you say the words *i love all of you. you're a fantastic human being*. and i know that you mean it. and my mind spins from the reality of how, once again, i have told you something i deem leave-worthy. i have laid at your feet a piece of my soul that i was so scared you would see and say *i just can't anymore*. and instead, you thank me for the gift.

and jesus christ i may still be learning what love is. but here, in these moments, stealing away from a party in an italian garden to listen to a voice note from your body two thousand miles away, somehow still feeling held by you, even when i was ready to drop.

maybe this, maybe this is what safe love truly is.

27 june 2024

tuscany

sometimes i miss you when the wind blows

some part of me

still wants

some part

    of you.

i don't think it would be fair

to say you

    could not

love me

the way i need

to be loved.

but i know you

    would not

love me

the way i need

to be loved.

you tell me she's wonderful,
and i know that it's true.
thing is, it's not her.
it's all about you.

how you've got me here,
yours for the taking.
but instead i just find
i'm in the wings waiting.

thing is, it's not you.
it's all about me.
and the thing is,
i kept the mono in non-monogamy.

i don't know if that's telling
or if it's just A Thing.
but, thing is, i've never really
been one to swing.

and no that's not quite true,
look back and you'll see,
it's often quite poly,
the amor that's in me.

i suppose that it matters,

who's on the other side.

when shallow, it's fluid,

can change with the tide.

but when deeper, it's different.

channels opened, now close.

can i share what's been given?

soul only knows.

6 july 2024
barbados

and suddenly

somehow

in one single instant

you have become

entirely human

once more.

7 july 2024
barbados

i take pictures of my body that i never send to you.

wanted you to want them,
    but you didn't want me
    enough.

how easy it would have been for you,
to waltz in and take it all.

all you'd have had to do
    was ask.

and all of it
would have been
yours.

you don't need me anymore
and i suppose that was the whole point.

for us not to need each other anymore.

but you not needing me
	before i stopped needing you
rests heavy in me.

circles around my mind
and pulls at the threads of ego
that want to wonder
	why.

22 july 2024
barbados

there is a hole in my heart the shape of you and the only thing i can do about it is love it.

love this empty space that helped expand what was already so expansive. hold it in my hands and smile at how i could have ever been without it.

love the fact that this shadow has now become part of me, too. even when it aches. even when it feels like no other could fill such a space. and no other will fill such a space.

but i will find room for more holes.

you left your mark on me in ways i never could have anticipated.

but nothing that truly makes life worth living

can ever be

anticipated.

july 2024
barbados

when he told me we could watch *the matrix* together someday and hold each other in bed for as long as we wanted, i believed him.

i clung to that future and i didn't watch *the matrix* even when i wanted to because i believed he believed in that far-off someday together as much as i did.

and i do believe he meant it, in the way people sometimes mean things they feel but don't think. or think but don't feel.

i suppose i needed to learn, just one more time, that i could never wait to do something i wanted because someone else said it wasn't time yet.

that i could never again wait for myself at the hand of another's timeline.

i had to feel that stretching and pulling and pining

just one more time

so i could learn,

once and for all,

that my desires

    wait

     for no one.

july 2024
barbados

i will not wait for you.
but i will always be here
if you are ready
to catch up.

8 january 2025

mexico city // *queensland*

you will take her to places we went to first
    and i will wonder if you think about me.

five hours later i will get a text from you
    of a picture of you
    in exactly one of those places
    with her.

and i will smile for how much
    i am still connected to you,
    all these moons later.

2010

2011

2012

2013

2014

2015

2016

2017

2018

2019

2020

2021

2022

2023

2024

22

20 july – 29 august 2024

barbados

> *for #22, who taught me that sometimes*
> *it's really just not that complicated*

12 august 2024
barbados

last night i was on top of the man who's filling space while i have it. the man who has been allowing me to explore places within myself through bringing out pieces within him. the man who is a complete blank slate. and while i was watching him—eyes closed, mind lost, feeling my body around his—he became you. suddenly every feature. every line. the colors of each hair of his beard. the hair covering his chest. the width of his nose. the contentedness on his face. all of him.

was you.

august 2024
barbados

we spend a month playing

    and exploring each others unknown.

me, pushing the limits

    you didn't know existed.

you, surprising me

    every time

    you allowed yourself

    to rise

    and meet me.

you were drunk when you picked me up and i didn't realize it until halfway to the restaurant. it had been a month of three nights a week with you inside of me and sitting in that car seat silently seething was the most you'd ever made me feel. but the thing was, you were so happy. and you were so you, just even more so. and that's how you always were. just exactly, totally, completely who you are.

i really do know you meant no malice with it. that it hadn't even occurred to you that it wouldn't be okay. coming to get me after however many rum punches with your friends. that's just what people do on the island, and you'd been there long enough to have let yourself assimilate to more than just the beach at sunset.

i told myself we'd have a long dinner and you would sober up and if it came down to it, i'd just drive the car home. but when we sat down to eat you ordered another drink and i braced myself to have the conversation it would have just been easier to not have to have, if you hadn't put me in the position of needing to have it.

but the drink never came. they simply forgot it.

and you let it go.

and even that was a lesson.

you, this space for me to practice using my voice. you, this person who heard me and allowed me and were safe enough to explore with while never risking getting lost.

you, without even knowing it, teaching me how to observe, and steady, and prepare, and let go.

learning, once more, that sometimes you simply must allow things to sort themselves out without ever needing to intervene.

august 2024
barbados

you were so straightforward

    it was almost jarring.

safe, sturdy, grounded.

entirely alien to the landscapes i brought you to,

and yet entirely willing to explore the new territory.

you were so receptive to my openness

    it became a game.

how far could i push this,

    how bold could i be?

but every door i opened,

    you'd peer inside.

and of every piece of me i showed you,

    not one made you hide.

14 september 2025
finsbury park, london

a year and a month after we had to go to the pharmacy together you resurface in my life. and even though i've long since come to stop expecting anything on this journey, i must say i really was not anticipating that.

i awaken to a message from you, sent past midnight your time. you were at the show of a band i'd introduced you to and, even though you said they were great, i read in your words an ache i had never felt from you before. an ache that said something fundamental in you had shifted.

an ache, i did not know then, that would serve as the fodder for igniting something true.

your message finished with the words *thank you for the influence you still have on my life*. and in that most sincere of sentences, you'd unknowingly written us a prophecy that has reopened the most beautifully unexpected of doorways.

7 november 2025

shoreditch, london

you were lacking a depth that honestly part of me hoped you'd never find. a depth that comes from having known grief in a way that leaves a cavern in your heart you will spend the rest of your life trying to understand. a camaraderie shared by those who've walked through hell and survived it. even if they would have rather burned alive, than have survived it.

you'd had an ease that only comes from ease. from a loose awareness that things have been smooth but an inability to grasp what the other side feels like.

and then a year later it shattered. and the floor dropped out from beneath you. and love brought you to new heights and her subsequent departure catapulted you into an abyss you'd heard of for decades like it was some far-off land that you'd never cared to see, but suddenly found yourself marooned in.

you reached out to me, from this new terrain. reopened the door. knew i had spent a lifetime exploring the universe you now called home. and although i would have done anything to have saved you from the pain you were in, there is a truth and a depth to our friendship that's blossomed in the soil of your heartache. a truth and a depth to who we've now become together, grown from a seed we didn't even know we were planting. a seed of shared experience, shared honesty. a shared care that we had both always upheld, even when we thought it had been so obvious our moment together was fleeting.

2010

2011

2012

2013

2014

2015

2016

2017

2018

2019

2020

2021

2022

2023

2024

17

october 2017 – october 2018

march 2019 – august 2019

and for lifetimes after that

earth

for #17, who taught me everything

10 december 2024

mexico city

you still come to me in dreams, only it's different now. last night i saw you at dinner with your new girlfriend and we all left at the same time and i don't know where you went but she and i crossed paths. i knew who she was but she didn't know me and we started talking and she was really incredible, this newfound lover of yours. we walked together for a while and it felt wrong not to tell her who i am but the moment never appeared and all i remember thinking is

wow she really is so wonderful.

and that she deserved better than you.

but how do you say that to even the most intimate of strangers? even in a dream? i could see her holding herself back for you, and wanted so badly to tell her to break free.

we kept walking together and it felt strange to me, how she didn't seem to realize she'd lost you. she was so content to wander alongside me, this seeming-stranger who'd just appeared. and i, the one of us wondering where you'd gone. wondering if she would even think to miss you.

some dark part of me wanted you to see us together. wanted to see the look on your face. but as she spoke i felt all of that fade. felt myself simply want to love her. want to tell her she could do better.

do better, even though you were so good.

wanted to tell her that i knew—so intimately, i knew—that it was that very goodness that would make it so hard for her to break free.

and it's funny, now. writing this out.

realizing, in real time, what it all means.

how she is me and i am her and i sit here six years later looking back knowing i deserved better but watching that version choose to stay because she did not yet truly believe she deserved better. even though she could feel the spirit of the future walking next to her, silently letting her know she is not alone.

incapable of speaking it aloud, but sending it in dreams, sending it in love, sending it in any way i can.

you deserve better.

you will set yourself free.

you will someday walk so lovingly alongside yourself. and realize you have been right here all along.

realize that i

have been alongside me

all along.

sometimes i wonder if you still love me
    the way i still love you.
not in the way i did, then.
but in the way i do, now.
in a way that is soft and gentle and reaches across space and time to touch your heart whenever you dance through my mind.
    in a way that says
        i hope you're happy.
        i hope you found your peace.
        i hope you are able to think of me,
            and think of love.
            and think of what we shared.
            and smile at the magic
                we once knew.

the most beautiful gift
he ever gave me

was letting me
go.

2010

2011

2012

2013

2014

2015

2016

2017

2018

2019

2020

2021

2022

2023

2024

2025

23

11 december 2024 – 8 january 2025

22 september 2025

23 – 24 november 2025

mexico city

toronto

london

for #23, who taught me ease

we meet on feeld and i tell you i'm just looking for friends and you say that's entirely fine and we both really do mean it when we say it.

the next day we go for coffee and spend eight hours tracing the threads of our timelines back through space, to every moment we'd unwittingly been in the same place on earth before today. as the dots through our inadvertently shared history connect, you take out your phone. and there on your screen is my face. in a sea of one hundred thousand strangers, taken two hundred and ninety-eight days prior, eight thousand four hundred and twenty-three miles away from where we now sat.

the invisible strings reveal themselves repeatedly, and we marvel in stoic wonderment as the tessellate unfurls before us.

melbourne, lyon, chasing each other through northern california in the summer of 2020.

feet apart, at times. but not able to see. not until today.

you spend the next month showing me the city that raised you, bringing me to the nooks and crannies you have loved long before the tiktok stars deemed it all *cool*.

and it's all just easy, being with you.

that ease lends itself to trust, and in the lead up to christmas the conversation opens—exploration, with love. a container to hold each other and meet each other and see what more there is to see.

and once the holiday has passed, we do just that.

with the depth and the honesty i had come to require, i step once more, into the arms of someone i knew i could trust to hold me.

31 december 2024

mexico city

on new years eve i bought secondhand heels and wore a dress i'd owned for eons, knowing it was all going to end up in a heap on your bedroom floor anyway.

our fancy dinner reservation fell through but we managed to squeeze into an invisible table at an italian spot i knew, and none of it really mattered because we were always going to be home by nine.

and home by nine we were, heels and dress strewn as i knew they'd be, bare bodies on your mattress, staring into each others eyes for minutes on end before our bodies even touched. just breathing. just being.

at 11:57 i was naked in your arms and you said *what should we do for midnight* and i said *do you think you can make me come right as the clock strikes twelve* and you said you'd do all you could to make it happen and all you could, you did.

they say how you start a year is how you spend it, and 2025 started in a fit of laughter.

the alarm we'd set for the bell toll going off when i was seconds away from the edge, both of us cracking up the moment the moment cracked.

you, abandoning all you could do to come up to kiss me and hold me as the year began.

me, knowing no matter what the future held, it would be held with the love it deserved.

i pull my naked body away from his
    and he asks where i'm going.
i say i just need to close the closet doors
    before we go sleep
        because spirits
        come in
        through closets
and he says
    that makes sense
    as though it really does.

8 january 2025

mexico city

after a month of effortlessness, the shared restlessness of our feet
carry us back out

    into our lives.

you, to europe and the adventures that called.

me, to chicago for a final farewell.

the transition, uncomplicated.

the friendship, unmoving.

the evolution, as natural as anything living could be.

the night after i leave you i sleep on the floor. laminate sheets made to look like hardwood; my body directly on the sterility of it all.

maybe i needed to feel something cold and dead to juxtapose the warmth and softness of you.

maybe i'm just the type of person who sleeps on the ground now.

i hadn't expected the weight that came, after just ten hours with you. hadn't expected you, but there we were. in the same city as one another for the first time in nine months. a change of flight and a missed connection ending me up on your doorstep at two o'clock in the morning. ending me up in your arms once again.

i'd said since before we'd last parted that maybe our relationship was changing, maybe i was changing. maybe the physical was giving way to devotional. maybe the next time, it wouldn't be the same.

and you had accepted that. the moment i told you our bodies may never touch in that most intimate of ways again, you had said the words *my love for you remains unchanged*.

i didn't know how desperately i had needed to hear a human being say that to me, until the words floated into my ears. how much the pure, unwavering acceptance of me as i am—with no expectation on the role my body would play in the matter—mattered. a trail of men had stayed as our dynamics had evolved and that in itself had healed so much. but the act of confessing it to you, of having it heard and held in real time with not an atom shifting in the way you loved me, that changed something deeper.

i had been in cars and in airports and on airplanes for nineteen hours and yet when i made it to your couch in the middle of the night, my legs in your lap, all weariness faded. we stayed up for hours just talking, just being with one another again. and when the sun was about to consider rising, i started slipping into that childlike state i get to when exhaustion finally consumes. you helped me up and brought me to bed. we stripped down to our underwear and climbed under the covers, where i still fit so perfectly into the curve of your protection.

earlier that evening, when it had truly become apparent that the fates were bringing me to you that night, i'd told you what i needed was just to be held. that my heart was tired and my body had been mine alone since i'd last seen you, and mine alone it was likely to remain. you'd said your arms awaited me and you'd wrap them around me as long as happenstance would allow and, for you, that would be enough.

and that's what you did.

you let me climb in and you wrapped me tight and we laid there together just being.

after an eternity in your arms had passed and i had melted into the safety of you once again, i asked in the softest voice if you would massage me, if you would use your hands to work out the weights that i still carried. and with devotion, you obliged. crawled out from under the warmth of those blankets and used your palms and your fingers and your strength to knead and to caress this body of mine that had felt no such touch since our last meeting.

after a second eternity in your grasp had relaxed me even more deeply into your refuge, i asked in a voice even softer if you would bring your hands where i'd told you they'd been unlikely to go. if you would bring your mouth there with them.

and you said *are you sure* and i said *yes* and you said *then of course.*

the place you brought me to split time.

universes appearing, visions flowing. worlds so far beyond me and pieces that dwelled so far within.

in the aftermath i was immobilized. you'd witnessed that moment so often before and even with the intensity of all of those precursors, you knew something about this had been different. something about these screams and these convulsions and the way i had grabbed your wrists had been unlike anything you'd brought out in me before.

with your hands still gripping me and your eyes locked on mine you asked if i was alright. the softness of my voice had all but turned to silence, yet i managed to tell you i might start to cry, and it might be the kind of cry that seemingly will never cease. you said that was okay and that you've got me and you came up to envelop my body in your embrace once again, to hold me in a way that said *you are safe, you can let it all go.*

but something in me kept the dams from breaking. some tiniest layer holding on from fullest release. you, so sturdy and so loving and so right. and still, an invisible thread holding me back. enough, in that moment, to have simply said the words and once again have them met with nothing other than *you can be exactly who you are, and that will be okay.*

we woke up in the same position we had fallen asleep in—your right arm still under my head, your left wrapped around the front of me, my arms and fingers intertwined through your grasp. you had promised to hold me, and there you were. keeping your word even as we'd dreamt.

as our bodies stirred we allowed what had opened the night before to carry us, to explore the territory i had thought might be closed. you felt familiar and human and present and while you held me beneath you, bodies unified, your eyes fixed on mine, you told me, so simply, that you loved me. and i told you, so simply, i loved you, too.

and even in that moment, that most tender and true moment, the words flashed through my mind:

this is not enough.

it was everything it ever could have been, and still. it was not enough.

and that was what i had needed to come here, unknowingly, to find. to experience, once again, what these depths felt like and to know, once more, how much deeper there was yet to go.

we got dressed and went to brunch at one of those north american diners where the potatoes are cubes and the coffee never ends. when the afternoon came you brought me to the train that would take me north to montreal, to laminate floors and technicolor treetops and the space for me to sit in the wake of it all.

and there, in that tiny studio on rue saint-denis, feeling loved and feeling hollow, not knowing what else to do, i lay on the floor.

i feel the veneer beneath me and the invisible weight of you above me.

and i wonder how something that appears so real from every possible angle, can still feel lifeless to the touch.

grey skies and melancholy.

a heaviness that rests behind my eyes.

tears that ask to flow

and a heart that knows not

    for what it yearns.

a heart that knows exactly

    for what it yearns.

this body, sacred space.

held with such love.

and still, not enough.

still not enough.

23 — 24 november 2025
london

three countries; eleven months.

pure happenstance; not a moment planned.

the revolution, in our evolution.

how love changes
how love remains.

you are the proof before the pudding.
the ease before the effortless.
the tell before the tale.

it is remarkable, how unremarkable it is with you.
extraordinary, how ordinary.

impossible, just how possible.

2010
2011
2012
2013
2014
2015
2016
2017
2018
2019
2020
2021
2022
2023
2024
2025

21

9 – 19 march 2023

17 – 23 march 2024

and so far beyond

december 2025

goa, india

east coast, australia

earth

east coast, australia

for #21, who taught me it really is possible to hold it all

12 december 2025

surfers paradise

yesterday, six hundred and thirty-two days after the morning you broke me and held me on the floor of that surfers paradise apartment shower, we saw each other for the first time since that week.

we got ice cream at the exact same place we had that afternoon, recreated the selfie we'd taken.

this time, with your sparkling partner smiling next to us in the frame.

she is beautiful in ways i know you had never known, before us.

she is healthy in ways you had never allowed yourself to experience.

and although i am happy for you, so happy for you, i cannot help but feel

      that the life you have chosen in our wake

      is an existence where your soul

         remains,

           insidiously,

         asleep.

25 december 2025

sunshine coast

it's christmas day and we're spending it together at your house.

at your house in the country you now live in. the country that has pulled me back to her lands, again and again. the country you first fell in love with alongside me. the country you moved to with the woman who came after you and i had played and loved and been free here, together.

when night has fallen, we find ourselves in your sunroom. away from everyone else, for just a moment. and i ask you how you're faring, being presented with the mirror of me. i've felt your energy adjusting all day, reacclimating to being near me again, as mine has been doing with you. and you say to be honest, it's a bit more confronting than you'd remembered. more jarring than you'd really been prepared for. you'd almost forgotten what it was like, staring yourself in the face through staring at me.

and i say *i know*.

when you've found what you're looking for in the dregs of the esky, we sit together on the sofa i will later spend the night sleeping on. you say *it's really good to see you*. and you say it in that way people do when they mean so much more than just those words. in a way that says they'd forgotten something sacred, but seeing you has made them realize all they've lost.

and, again, i say *i know. it's really good to see you, too.*

you tell me how the life you've built is incredible. a dream come true. the friends, the adventure, the love. how, in so many ways, it's everything a person could ever want. everything you told yourself you needed.

but still, you wondered.

still, even in the moments that were so seemingly picturesque, sometimes the words would float through your mind:

this is not enough.

it was everything it ever could have been. and maybe, it wasn't enough.

the thing is, i had nearly convinced myself over the course of the last year and a half that you really had accepted this. that you really had chosen the life that exists within the lines we think we're meant to want. that you had forgotten the magic i had seen you taste in india and in cornwall and in byron bay and you had decided on a different way. and accepting your acceptance had allowed me to free myself of the *you* i had felt, for so long, on some other plane.

the *you* i had hoped, for so long, you may someday become.

but here you were, admitting to me that you still knew.

that you still felt the pull.

that the voice that lures *maybe there is more* had not stopped singing.

and wouldn't you know how solacing it felt, hearing you say that?

and wouldn't you know how maddening it became, hearing the truth whispered aloud?

and wouldn't you know how readily my heart jumped on it, the idea that someone i loved yearned for something greater.

but it was a pattern of mine, don't you see? wanting a life for you that you had not chosen yourself.

it was a pattern of mine, i assure you, hoping my presence could inspire a different path.

it was a cage of mine, most treacherous, looking my future in the eye and desperately trying to bring someone along when they'd already ardently chosen to remain.

it just kind of happened.

we woke in the morning to your living room full of friends strewn about the floor and my heart tumbled at the magic of this life. thirty-four years old, waking up at your house after a christmas together. everyone telling stories and lounging in the morning light.

and, suddenly, there i was.

living one of those mornings. with you.

i stole away and facetimed my family next to the pool, and you came over and joined. as you entered the frame, my mom made a comment about how cute you are and asked if you had a girlfriend.

and, suddenly, there we were.

with my family on christmas. my mom absolutely smitten by you in an instant.

the others dwindled out the door and into their days, and i stayed. under no guise, under no pretense. just you, and me, and the morning your girlfriend had told us to enjoy together as she'd left for work. after she'd spent her christmas day with me, telling me she knows how much i mean to you and how happy she was to finally meet me.

and, suddenly, there we were.

truly alone together for the first time in nearly two years.

you suggested we go back to lay on the patio sofa as we'd been doing all morning and said i could wear as much or as little as i felt comfortable in.

i peeled my own layers back as i walked.

and then, suddenly, there we were.

standing naked in front of one another on your terrace. bodies remembering each other, old habit creeping to life.

you said we should shower, and as we walked inside together we laughed about how neither of us had foreseen this happening, as preposterous as that sounds now. but it really had seemed, up until that moment, like maybe this era of ours had passed. like maybe we really had laid it to rest.

but then, there we were.

in a shower together. pressed up against tile once more, bubbles down the drain, my whole body shaking for an entirely different reason from what had shaken me that morning in surfers paradise. that morning, lifetimes ago, that now felt as close as you.

sufficiently cleansed and uninterested in standing, i said *let's go to the living room*. body still wet, you threw me a towel and to the living room we went.

you made a nest on the ground of blankets and pillows, put down a sheet to catch the blood. little about this act would be devotional, but we joked about scenes and sacrifice replaying across time.

you felt familiar and foreign and comforting and wrong and somehow i thought it would have been easier, had it just been earth-shatteringly clear the moment we touched that this was it. that we were back in the current we had stepped out of so long ago.

but that, i've learned, is not how these things go.

the barriers were as much spiritual as they were physical, but still, we met one another. and still, we were so far apart.

in that between space, when bodies are resting but the air between them remains palpably electric, i sat on top of you, hands on your chest. i told you this moment did not count as the real conversation—that there would come a time when we would have it deliberately—but i could not let pass what you'd brought up the night before. in hushed tones and in a room away from everyone else, the pull you'd said that still existed. the life, about which, you still wondered.

a life of freedom. a life untethered.

nothing to do with me, and yet my presence elicited the speaking of it. my being, drawing it from heart to voice.

your morning mind was less fluid than that of the evening prior. and although you met me in the sincerity and honesty i have come to hold as standard from you, the daylight and shift in consciousness betrayed in you a doubt. a veil that spoke over truth.

you asked me what i thought, even though, you said, you knew what i thought.

and i said, *darling what you think i think is simply what you already know yourself.*

i told you you had two paths ahead of you. one, where you listen. where you set yourself free. even if it hurts. and, oh beautiful boy, it will hurt.

the other, where you don't. where you pretend *this is enough*. in that future, i said, the longing will not cease. it will call and call and call to you in the back of your mind for eons. until one day, after years of implorations have gone unlistened to, that voice will silence. and on that day, your soul will die.

it will not hurt because it will not feel. but it will kill you.

the choice, beloved, is yours, i tell you.

and you look at me with the eyes you use when you know i am right.

and you speak to me with the voice you use when you are fooling yourself.

and you say you aren't sure.

and you say you just don't know.

26 december 2025

sunshine coast

we go to brunch afterwards and you ask me how the book is going and i say *i'm finishing it now* and then i remind you that you are my biggest mirror.

you say *i know*.

and i say *the parts about you are pretty intense*.

and you say *that makes sense*.

we talk about my dreams and how i'm doing everything i knew i'd do.

and i feel in you a hollowed vacancy,

>a void that still fills me

>with anguished yearning.

27 december 2025
queensland

i love you in a way

i do not love

any

other

being.

on boxing day you left bruises across the back of me. black and blue smudges the shape of your teeth punched along my ribs; fingerprints dug into my backside. the metaphors write themselves, it seems.

two days later i send you a message. inviting you, once more, into this life with me. reminding you that the door has stayed open. telling you i know, that with me, it is a lot. that i ask things of you that no one else does. that the path i walk is no easy one, but for you, i believe, it is right. that your journey is your own, but here i sit. ready to welcome you, if you're ready to welcome yourself.

and you, yet again, choose to remain. choose the mortal plane and the existence you can feel you've outgrown.

it breaks me anew, your refusal to join me. how the mirror i hold for you makes you cower instead of rise.

and i, once again, find myself feverishly praying you'll wake up and come meet me,

even when you've shown me

tirelessly

where you've chosen

to stay.

december 2025
queensland

if you truly feel that seeing me is not what's meant for you and your path right now,

i entirely respect that.

if you're just scared that spending time with me would mess up your entire life,

well then, darling, your entire life is already messed up.

and it has nothing

to do

with me.

december 2025
queensland

467

it has nothing

to do

with you

and everything

to do

with freedom.

29 december 2025
queensland

i don't take scraps
   from anyone.

and yet
   i beg for them
      from you.

i don't know how it's possible that you ignoring the song of your heart can hurt me the way it does. how you simply living the way you choose to live can feel like my own soul is taking a beating. it frankly drives me mad in a way i have never known, watching you decide to stay trapped.

i trust it entirely.

and still
　　it feels
　　　　like daggers
　　in my eternity.

i trust it entirely.

and still
　　it wrings through me
　　　　so deeply
　　　　i can barely
　　　　　　breathe.

you chose to stay human and after you i chose humans

    because the taste of immortality

    had not yet dissipated.

but here i am, drinking ambrosia again.

    inviting you, once more,

    to plunge with me

    into the styx.

30 december 2025

queensland

do this fury and heartache

    stem

    from some far-off future

    in which you have chosen differently?

    in which i can feel

    our tendrils

    re-intertwine?

or do this fury and heartache

    burn through me

    simply for witnessing

    and recognizing

    a soul

      as massive as ours

    choosing

      a life

      that is not

        true?

i truly and entirely trust it all.

and it feels

    like my entire being

      is dying.

it would be a bold-faced lie to say i didn't scream into the night for over a week, after just one morning entwined with you.

it caught me off guard, how much you caught me.

how laying it all at your feet and having you pick nothing up drove me to a madness i'd believed had long left me.

it took days to realize you were the final test, the reckoning of what would be.

go back into the hedge maze of my own shadows?

keep myself trapped in the cage of my own making?

or truly, once and for all,

> step into the unending clarity
>
> of my own light?

i came here to finish the story

and i hadn't even known

    it was yet left

        to end.

31 december 2025

queensland

another australian december with a doorway ajar.

another australian december with lunacy setting in by months end.

a different coast,

a new storyline.

this time, i see.

this time, i commit

to me.

1 january 2026
queensland

how you start a year is how you spend it, and 2026 started with me. in the bush in queensland. five am wake up, alone in the dreamscape mirage of the future i had for so long seen. setting every vision i'd ever had for myself ablaze. further igniting the places in me that were already roaring with life.

knowing, in a way that is no longer capable of being contained, that my voice would never again falter as she bridged the realms between what had been felt and what was known.

that now, the deepest truths of my experience

were ready to free themselves

from my soul.

january 2026
queensland

i always knew that letting you go
would mean stepping into forever.
that letting you go
would begin the life i had moved toward
since time began.

you're a mirror and i know that.
but if that's truly all you are
     then how can it possibly feel this way?
i know it doesn't matter.
     even if it matters more than anything.
because no matter what you are,
     i know
all i can do
     is go.
all i can do is continue to walk this path.
all i can do is never turn back.
all i can do
     is everything
i came here to do
     all along.

i don't believe you.

i don't.

not when you say you're happy,

not when you say this is enough.

i don't believe your soul is alive

    and i don't believe for a second that you

    truly fucking believe it either.

i've seen the light when it floods your eyes

    but darling it's been darkness for years.

you keep saying just one more thing *until*

and it's an until that never comes.

until until until

until when, my darling?

until what, my love?

until you've smothered that yearning

    so far down inside of you

    that you can no longer hear her sing?

un till the barren dirt you've buried her in.

un till the lifeless ground where you've recklessly shrouded your soul.

i will be here when you are ready.

i will help tend your neglected earth

    into richest soil.

but until then

    i will till my own eden

    alone.

i dream i'm in a house with my family and the dog i was watching escaped and you came over and we started to have sex and you called out the fact that last time was a bit shit and if we were going to do it we needed to do it right.

we went upstairs for privacy and my room was a mess and there was no door in the frame and i was trying to clean but i felt no guilt or shame or frenzy over the chaos of my life all over the floor.

i said *you know how sometimes you just throw everything everywhere* and you said *yeah* but i knew you didn't really know.

in the middle of all of it i met with a healer about a soreness in my throat and she didn't even need to tell me it was already mended for me to know i had healed it.

and then i was driving on a road and every exit was blocked and a man i did not know told me i could not leave and i just looked at him and i left.

the road turned to one made of rainbow-colored broken glass and the shards filled the tires and it felt like art, not danger, collecting these jagged technicolor fragments in the wheels that carried me.

and through the whole dream, i just felt calm.

there were turns and hiccups and lost dogs and messes and shattered glass and i navigated it and it was all art and i knew peace.

at the end i awoke to a voice in my mind cooing the words,

you've got a lot of things to do, little girl.

and i do.

and isn't that just the most wonderful thing

you have ever heard?

january 2026
queensland

everything single thing
i have ever thought or felt
    about you
is simply the very thing
    i believed
    and felt
        about myself

the wind blows and a sadness tires.
in this moment, a feeling
    that i really may never see you again.
not mine to know
    what she means as she whispers.
you, as you are now.
or you, as you will never choose
    to be.

the most beautiful gift
i ever gave myself

was setting myself
   free.

whenever

wherever

∞

i am so grateful to the men

who have let me go.

who have set me free

even when they wanted

to keep me.

who have been able to see

that my devotion to them

was impeding my devotion

to my own soul.

who knew that we were both trapped

so long as my path remained tangled.

who have broken both of our hearts

in the name of freeing mine.

i am grateful beyond words.

and i am so sorry

if your heart

got caught

in the crossfire

of my rewilding.

∞

thank you for showing me
what is possible
thank you for showing me
i deserve
so much
more.

∞

all i have ever wanted is to show you my world. to hold it out with cusped palms, saying *here, look at this. isn't it beautiful?*

all i have ever wanted is for you to take one minute, just one minute, to sit with me in awe and wonder. to look magic in the eye and say *i see you*.

for years i tried to bring you in

    and for years you chose to stay.

and so i learned to venture alone. to find the havens of heaven, the morsels of magic, the truth in the fairytales.

i built myself a universe of everything i knew could always be, and here i am

in paradise

entirely

    free.

∞

the kind of eyes that are looking for something.
the kind of eyes that you've almost convinced yourself
no longer exist.

and then suddenly,
    there they are.

staring at you
    with those eyes.

and in an instant you know:
    your whole world
    has just
    changed.

Lindy Ehemann spent her childhood living in Hong Kong, Germany, and the suburbs of Chicago. Her early years were painted in a mosaic of different cultures, sights, tastes, and sounds that overlaid an inner world just as vibrant and complex as the one around her. Deeply emotional, pensive, and reflective from birth, Lindy was set on discovering all this human experience has to offer from the day she arrived.

She lived for decades with this simultaneous insatiable thirst for life, while carrying a deep emotional and spiritual weight that manifested in inner unrest and an unrelenting search for answers. That quest to heal her heart and come home to herself led to her moving and traveling around the world in search of expansion and growth.

She spent her twenties living in Madison, Wisconsin; Paris; London; Melbourne, Australia; Queenstown, New Zealand; New York City; and Chicago, along with backpacking foreign soil for months on end. She worked endless hours bartending to save money to jump ship again, always called by the voice in her heart that told her she *must* go.

Psychedelics played a major role in her spiritual and emotional journey in her later twenties, helping expand her consciousness and open doors she'd long held closed. It was her first experience with ayahuasca—just four days after her thirtieth birthday—that revealed she could no longer live in the patchwork life she'd forced herself into for decades.

At thirty, she finally committed herself to facing every ghost that dwelled within her, chasing her wildest dreams, and truly setting herself free.

She left her life behind and spent four years traveling the world, led purely by her own intuition and heart. She ended up going back to nearly every place on earth she had ever been and saving the version of herself that had been there before: realizing that the voice she had always heard in her heart—the voice that urged her to keep going, even in the darkest nights—had always been her own, echoing from the future she now lived in. Living the story was the act that had written the story, and she had been her savior all along.

These intentional trips—both the external travels to places on earth, and the internal voyages through her own consciousness with the aid of psychedelics—came to be the method by which she healed her heart, saved her inner child, and finally set herself free.

At thirty-five, she is telling the full story of this journey home to herself. *words about* men is just the first piece of a tapestry that will weave together to show the entire universe of how all the moments and threads connected to bring her exactly where she was always heading.

The next book will begin with that first night with ayahuasca and the truly remarkable adventure that unfolded in the wake of finally committing to the life that always awaited her.

You can connect more deeply to her story and artwork at intentionaltrips.com. You can also support her story at Patreon.com/LindyE, where she is publishing her raw, unfiltered journals from her travels and healing journey—giving you full, unrestrained access to her inner world as she navigated her way back home.